Bournemouth
and the Battlefields

To

Brian

Best Wishes

Jenny Young

21. 6. 19

Bournemouth and the Battlefields

WW1 Memorabilia and its connection to the town

Jenny Young

Published by JY publications

© Copyright Jenny Young 2019

BOURNEMOUTH AND THE BATTLEFIELDS

ISBN 978-1-799-02116-2

Book formatted by www.bookformatting.co.uk.

Contents

Acknowledgements

With grateful thanks to Alwyn Ladell and Rod Arnold for allowing me to use their photos when I was at a loss. Also to Magsy Watton for her sterling proof reading work – I knew her obsession with punctuation would come in handy one day! My thanks also to Dave for adopting the role of Comma Policeman. Special thanks must also go to Mrs Elizabeth Edgington, for graciously allowing me to make use of her late husband Michael's work, without which much of the historical background would have been missing.

Finally, to all those family and friends who have supported my efforts over the past six years to ensure that the men and women of Bournemouth who were caught up in the conflict of the First World War are remembered – my love and thanks.

Items belonging to author's Grandfather,
Private Henry Herbert Troke, born Holdenhurst 1877,
served in Rifle Brigade & Hampshire Regiment
from 1914 -1919

To Dave
For Bringing the Sunshine

Introduction

Items connected with the First World War, are now a popular area for the collector and while some collections can rightly be called Militaria, including as they do artillery shells, battlefield relics and medals, this book is based around my personal collection of WW1 memorabilia that reflects the social history of the war. Many books have been published about the First World War; the reasons why it happened; the specific battles; survivor stories and the lessons learned, the majority scholarly works of military history. This book does not claim to be one such as those, but one which may appeal to anyone with an interest in WW1 and more specifically the effect the war had on the town of Bournemouth. Each of the items found within is linked to several themes pertinent to the social history of a seaside town during the war years, along with general First World War themes such as army life and postal services. Many of the objects also have a personal story to tell; stories of Bournemouth folk who lived or were lost during the years 1914 -1918.

Writing a book that deals with everyday life in Bournemouth during the period when it was very much a garrison town, would not be possible without including information contained in the seminal work of research *'Bournemouth and the First World War – The Evergreen Valley 1914 -1918' by M.A Edgington*. As the first work of non-fiction covering this period in Bournemouth's history, Michael Edgington's now scarce book is unparalleled in its content, and very much deserves to be reprinted and made accessible to a far wider audience. It is with the express approval and permission of Mrs Elizabeth Edgington, that some of the information contained in her late husband's work is included here. Hopefully, this will inspire those wishing to learn more, to hasten to their nearest library to borrow a copy or provide the impetus for a long overdue reprint.

By including the personal stories connected to some of the items, it is the intention of the author to remember just a few of the local men and women who, due to the timing of their birth, got caught up in one of the most catastrophic wars in history, but who by the sacrifice made or the humanity showed, created the world and the freedoms we take for granted today.

Jenny Young 2019

01 Fundraising Flag Day Pins

Fundraising: Life in the Town

Selling small paper or silk flags to raise money for various sections of the war effort is thought to have been the idea of Mrs Brysson Morrison, daughter of an Edinburgh lawyer who organised the first official Flag Day on 5 September 1914. Having first placed an advert in the *Glasgow Herald* with the request, 'Help those fighting for the colours by wearing the colours', half a million paper Union Jacks were produced for sale and thereby the Flag Day movement was established.

For that very first 'Union Jack Day' in Glasgow, 3,600 collecting tins were issued, and each collector carried a tray of the small flags that would sell for a minimum of one penny. The enthusiasm of the collectors, who included the Boys' Brigade decked out in red, white, and blue scarves, and a woman who got up at 5 a.m. to sell to workers on the night shift returning home, ensured this novel idea was a runaway success. After the official Union Jack flags sold out, the lady collectors started to cut up their own ribbons to create further supplies. Not to appear out of step with public opinion, very few people were seen who were not sporting a flag or ribbon to show their support. When the collecting tins were emptied the sum of £3,800 had been collected in just one day.

As the war progressed, so did the number of charitable causes the flags were sold to support, and designs became more varied than the initial replicas of national flags. The earliest flags were printed in multiples on sheets of paper or thin card, which were folded in

half with a pin placed in the crease. After the 'pinning', which was often done by school children, the halves would be glued together to form the flag.

Every town and city across the country held their own flag days for local causes, as well as joining in those nationally organised. By the end of the war the Flag Day movement could proudly boast that they had 'done their bit' by raising over twenty-five million pounds.

One of the first fundraising events supported by the Flag Day movement was the rather controversial 'Fag Day Fund'. Realising the importance of cigarettes and tobacco to both soldiers serving overseas and the wounded in hospitals across the country, on 29 October 1914, *The Times* announced that at Lord Kitchener's request a 'Smokes for Soldiers and Sailors Fund' had been set up. The distribution of free cigarettes did not meet with approval by those who maintained that smoking was detrimental to health, and opinion remained divided on the subject.

Some of the larger national campaigns included the YMCA Hut Fund Flag Day. To cope with new recruits, and those billeted in towns such as Bournemouth, the army erected tents on wasteland and in public parks. Some councils could not cope with the number of men forced on them, with the result that resources were stretched to breaking point, so the YMCA stepped in and offered help to replace the tents with huts made of timber and corrugated iron. The money raised from the local Flag Day paid for new huts to be erected in areas such as Winton and Pokesdown.

The part Bournemouth played in fundraising for others caught up in The Great War is acknowledged in *Serbia's Great War 1914-1918* by Serbian Historian Andrej Mitrovic, in which he states:

'The work of others dedicated to relieving Serbia's plight stretched across the country, encompassing 'flag days' in Glasgow, 'Serbian Weeks' in Bournemouth, and a collection of cash on the trams of Sheffield. By May 1915 £100,000 had been raised'

19 October 1919 saw one of the largest collecting days - Red Cross Flag Day. Thirty-two million flags were made for distribution across the country in two different designs, the humble card one selling at the usual 1d and an up-market silk version for 3d.

In Bournemouth, prior to the War Charities Act of 1916 making it illegal to raise money for charity unless registered and approved, numerous Flag Days were held seeking support and aid for the Polish (raising £735); the Russians (£671) and the French (£573). By 1917 there was no end to the eclectic range of worthwhile causes from Wounded Army Horses to War Zone Ambulances, all prevailing on the goodwill and sympathy of the public who themselves were struggling to make ends meet.

(Author's Collection)

'Sandbags Save Soldiers' Postcard

On 21 April 1917, Bournemouth's residents were encouraged to give generously in support of the Sick and Wounded Horses Fund after the *Bournemouth Graphic's* article on the plight of horses sent to the front. In response to this appeal, approximately 400 people of all ages took part in the street collection, raising the not inconsiderable sum of £660.

Despite the effort put into it, 'Sandbags for Soldiers' which took place in Bournemouth one Saturday in August 1915, did not prove as lucrative for the cause as was hoped. The members of the Women's Emergency Corps organised a parade of sandbag covered vehicles through the town, and a street collection to raise money to provide sandbags for use in the trenches. Of all the Flag Day collections, this one raised the least amount - £502. However, by the end of 1915, more than £5,000 in total had been collected by Flag Day sellers on the streets of Bournemouth and by the time the Flag Day committee held their final meeting in July 1919, a total of £28,000 had been raised from the thirty-six Flag Days organised.

Today, these small forerunners of the modern stickers given out at charity collections have their own group of dedicated collectors. Although over 100 years old, these fragile scraps of First World War ephemera can still be found in surprisingly good condition. However, what could once be purchased for the price of 1d, the equivalent of half a penny in today's money, will now cost the modern buyer anywhere between six pounds for a basic French Tricolour flag and forty pounds for a more scarce Aid for Jewish Refugees pin.

**'From the magnificent manner which the whole
Empire has responded to the call of the Motherland, I
decided that no more suitable emblem could be sold
than the Union Jack'**

Mrs Agnes Brysson Morrison

02 *Daily Mirror* – 14 August 1915

War Reporting: Aviation: Air War: RFC: Local Lives

The Royal Flying Corps had been established for less than three years by the outbreak of WW1 and the potential of aircraft for more than observation and reconnaissance work not fully realised. On 13 August 1914, sixty machines in three squadrons flew from Dover to join the British Expeditionary Force in France, and on 19 August the RFC undertook its first reconnaissance action of the war when two aircraft carrying just pilots took to the skies in poor weather above Mauberge.

However, as the war escalated armed aircraft supported the British Army. This led to aerial dog fights with pilots of 'Die Fliegertruppe' (Imperial German Flying Corps) resulting in incredible acts of bravery and heroism as the British pilots attempted not only to shoot down their opponents but to return to base with their lightweight, canvas covered machines intact.

Lieutenant Roland Henry Peck was born in Thetford, Norfolk on 21 May 1891, one of five children born to William and Emma, who by 1901 had moved to Harcourt Road in Pokesdown. From January 1904 until December 1905, Roland attended Bournemouth School, then situated in Portchester Road, but did not excel as a student in either academic studies or on the sports field. By 1911 Roland had left school and was employed as a travelling salesman.

Roland's service in World War I started with the announcement of his commission to the 5th Service Battalion, Dorsetshire Regiment in the *London Gazette* of October 1914. The Bournemouth school magazine, *The Bournemouthian*, reported later

THE DAILY MIRROR, Saturday, August 14, 1915

READ MR. BOTTOMLEY'S GREAT MESSAGE IN "SUNDAY PICTORIAL"

The Daily Mirror

CERTIFIED CIRCULATION LARGER THAN ANY OTHER PICTURE PAPER IN THE WORLD

No. 3,684 — Registered at the G.P.O. as a Newspaper. — SATURDAY, AUGUST 14, 1915 — One Halfpenny.

BRITISH AIRMAN WITH FIFTY WOUNDS IN HIS LEG: UNCONSCIOUS WHEN HIS MACHINE TURNED TURTLE.

Preparing to lift the officer out of the machine. The greatest care was necessary.

Just after landing. The observer is seated astride behind the pilot.

The doctor, who is wearing a cap, makes an examination of the leg.

The observer, who was unhurt, brings the injured pilot a glass of water.

A wonderful feat of endurance has been performed by a Royal Flying Corps officer. His leg was nearly severed by shrapnel while he was flying over the German lines, and he lost consciousness. His machine turned turtle, but afterwards righted itself, and as it slid to the pilot regained his senses. He then flew to an aerodrome he knew of and, despite his injuries, made a perfect landing. Though he had fifty wounds in his leg, the doctors hope to save it.

11

that Roland was one of the first of their old boys to obtain a commission and at the beginning of 1915 he transferred to the Royal Flying Corps as a Second Lieutenant. Before joining No 7 Squadron RFC as an observer at the base at St Omer in France on 20 February 1915, Roland paid a visit to his old school and to his headmaster Dr Fenwick.

St Omer had been an active airfield before the war, but in August 1914 became the point of arrival in France for the deploying RFC. Here, the 'Old Bournemouthian' would have enjoyed a life far removed from that of the life in trenches had he stayed with the Dorset Regiment. The squadron's mess was a local estaminet (café/restaurant), where the men could let off steam over a hearty meal whilst reading London newspapers. Hot water was in plentiful supply as was the local wine.

Second Lieutenant Peck's first taste of ariel combat was on 3 July 1915. While acting as an observer on a dawn reconnaissance, his aircraft was involved in fierce fighting over Armentieres. The combat lasted for twenty minutes and both Roland and his pilot were wounded by exploding cartridges before they managed to break away from the engagement. Although wounded in the skirmish, neither Roland nor his pilot sustained serious injuries.

It would be the dramatic action of the 31 July 1915 that captured the interest and imagination of the national press which resulted in Roland Peck from Bournemouth making the front page of the *Daily Mirror* on 14 August 1915 and earning him a Mention in Despatches.

On that Saturday morning in July, Roland was to act as an observer for the pilot Captain John Aidan Liddell, their orders being to fly their Royal Aircraft Factory RE5 2457, described by some pilots as resembling 'a blowsy old woman that floundered about in the sky', over the German lines, circling round Ostend and flying in an arc to Bruges and Ghent. Although take off was scheduled for 08.00 hrs, due to necessary repairs on the RE5, applying seven fabric patches to the top and bottom of the aircraft, Aidan (as he preferred to be known) and Roland did not get airborne till 09.15 hrs.

Flying at 5,000 feet they flew safely over the Belgian-held front line and on towards Ostend. Constantly scanning the sky for enemy aircraft, they set a course for Bruges during which time Roland unstrapped himself in order to increase his field of vision. Suddenly they came under heavy machine-gun fire from above, and Roland, spotting the enemy aircraft, fired off a full drum of ammunition before reloading in an attempt to take down the German two-seater. However, before he was able to do so disaster struck and the RE5 was hit by a burst of enemy gun fire causing an immediate nosedive. As Roland Peck later recalled, 'I had just reloaded when our machine nose-dived and then turned completely over, and all the remaining ammunition fell out'.

The resulting damage to the left-hand side of the aircraft was severe. The pilot, Aidan, had been badly wounded in his right leg and thigh causing him to lose consciousness, and as the aircraft flipped over it looked as if their war was all over. Roland, unstrapped in the back of the plane, clung on desperately, determined not to fall out of the spinning aircraft as he watched all the equipment and ammunition drop to the ground. Regaining consciousness, Aidan realised the peril they were in and valiantly fought to regain control and save the life of his observer Roland Peck. Later in hospital he made light of the dreadful situation by saying that, 'I thought it might be a good thing to straighten her out and recover flying position. Just as well I had that brainwave, what?' Using every bit of strength still in him and mindful of what needed to be done, Aidan got the badly damaged aircraft under control and despite plunging 3,000 feet brought the RE5 back up the right way and flying straight.

However, Aidan also knew that he was badly wounded, losing blood and that his strength would not last, so had to land the plane as soon as possible. While he could have settled for a crash landing behind enemy lines, knowing that the aircraft could come under further enemy fire, he was determined to land on friendly territory. They were now flying an aircraft with no throttle cable and a damaged rudder at around 2,000 feet. There was a prevailing wind to battle, but still Aidan was able to get the damaged machine to gain height and despite being subjected to further gunfire, crossed the enemy lines at 2,800 feet.

Communicating by means of a blackboard passed between them, Roland indicated that they should make for the airfield of La Panne near Furnes where they could hope to find much needed medical help for Aidan. In a badly damaged aircraft, with most of the controls shot away and steering with a damaged rudder cable, Captain John Aidan Liddell attempted the impossible. He had one chance to land the shattered aircraft. Timing his actions to perfection and having brought the RE5 low enough, he killed the engine and safely landed the plane.

On landing, Roland jumped from the aircraft and summoned assistance from the Belgians who were soon surrounding the damaged RE5. One, a photographer took a series of photos as events unfolded. Aidan realised that his leg was badly broken and that he had lost a great deal of blood. Reluctant to let unskilled rescuers pull him from the cockpit, he refused to move until a doctor arrived and in true 'Boy's Own' style fashioned a splint and applied a tourniquet. The photographer captured the moments when Roland stood guard over his injured pilot, keeping him from losing consciousness and handing him water until the medical team arrived and Aidan was finally gently lifted from the plane.

The incredible heroism and flying skills shown on that day so captured the interest of the public, both in England and Belgium, that the national newspapers published the story on 14 August using the photographs taken at the time. An RFC officer from Bournemouth had made front page news!

Sadly, although initial indications were that Captain Liddell was on the mend, his condition deteriorated suddenly. Despite an emergency amputation of the shattered leg and just after hearing that he was to be awarded the VC for his bravery, Captain John Aidan Liddell died on 31 August 1915.

Second Lieutenant Roland Henry Peck went on to undertake pilot training at the Central Flying School in Upavon, Wiltshire in September 1915, after attending Aidan's funeral on the 4 September representing No 7 Squadron and the RFC. After qualifying as a pilot on 1 October 1915, at the beginning of 1916 Roland joined No. 30 Squadron in the Middle East supporting the troops involved in the Mesopotamia Campaign. During the siege of Kut-al-Amara, (December 1915 - April 1916), when 11,800 British and Indian troops were besieged inside the garrison there, Roland's 30 Squadron dropped supplies and undertook reconnaissance work.

It was whilst carrying out reconnaissance on 5 March 1916, that Roland's Voisin VS1541 was shot down by a German aircraft over the Tigris. Roland and his crew member were killed and now lie somewhere in modern Iraq. In a letter sent home to Roland's father, by now living in Highfield Road, Moordown, Bournemouth, Major Smith writes the following:

'The aeroplane was brought down by the enemy's gunfire, and both officers were killed instantaneously. The enemy aviators dropped a message in our lines informing us of the fate of the two officers, and stating that this was the fortune of war. The loss of your son was greatly regretted by all ranks of the RFC; during his short period of service in Mesopotamia he had shown himself to be a competent and gallant pilot'

Roland Henry Peck is commemorated on the Basra Memorial, originally located on the quay at Maqil but moved in its entirety by presidential decree to a site thirty-two km from Nasiriyah. The climate of political instability has made it challenging for the Commonwealth War Graves Commission to maintain the site, although in 2018 they were able to inspect the memorial for the first time in twelve years.

Roland was awarded the 1914-15 Star, the British Medal and the Victory Medal with Oak Leaf denoting his Mention in Despatches and is one of the 118 local men remembered on the memorial in St John's Church, Moordown.

Roland Henry Peck

**'I know that I shall meet my fate, somewhere among
the clouds above'**

W B Yeats

03 WW1 Crested China

WW1 Souvenirs: Crested China: Local Retailers

Crested china had been a popular holiday souvenir since the mid-1800s, when holiday makers of all ages and class were able to purchase a reminder of their holiday, or even a national event for a few shillings. The craze for collecting these small decorative items saw no sign of abating, and although W H Goss was almost certainly the first manufacturer to see the potential, by the 20th Century almost all other potteries in Stoke-on-Trent were producing their own range. Today the pieces made by Goss are those most sought after.

When war broke out in August 1914, the china manufacturers saw nothing wrong in capitalising on the patriotic spirit of the day and the enthusiasm of the market and began to introduce a wide range of crested china that replicated in miniature the militaria and accessories of war. As the war raged on, there seemed to be no end to the variety of new models based on the personalities and technological advances that reflected the progress of the war and those fighting in it. One advert in *The Pottery and Glass Record,* February 1919 for Arcadian China proudly boasts, 'Over 500 shapes. Comprising latest Military novelties'.

Figures – Willow China began producing their models of soldiers and sailors inscribed with, 'Our Brave Defender' just a few months into the war, and this range was later extended to include an airman and a nurse. Arcadian China, one of the most prolific makes of crested china, quickly followed suit with twelve busts of military

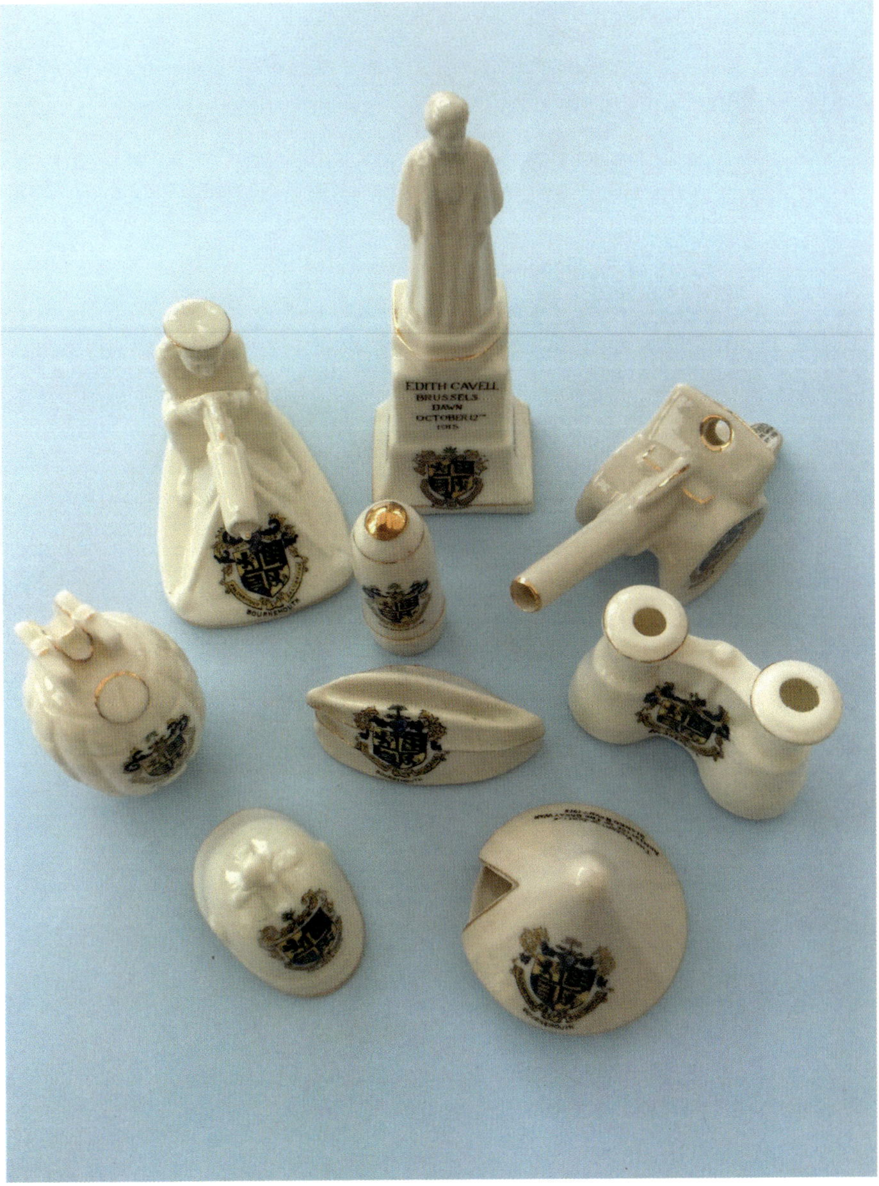
EDITH CAVELL
BRUSSELS
DAWN
OCTOBER 12TH
1915
BOURNEMOUTH

personnel and sixteen figures adopting questionably realistic poses.

'Tommies' were made standing to attention, firing guns, on horseback and even in dugouts. Sailors and Nurses were not left out, as the pottery companies vied for their share of the growing market.

Personalities included Lord Kitchener, King George V, and Sir John French, although perhaps the most poignant being that of Nurse Edith Cavell, produced after the war as a memorial figure to the brave nurse executed by German firing squad on 12 October 1915.

Tommies Kit – Many models produced come under this heading and do not just replicate those items associated with a British Soldier, but also those of other nations. The majority of factories introduced into their range colonial hats and French and German helmets in addition to officers' caps, Glengarrys, forage caps and pith helmets of the British Forces. Bell tents, bugles, field glasses and daggers are just some of the items that were produced not only with the crest of a particular town but also with that of a regiment, although some of the models available, such as the trench lamp and dagger were not standard army issue in reality.

Artillery – All the main manufacturers, such as Willow, Savoy, Arcadian and Carlton, produced a selection of the type of field gun and mortar now associated with WW1. Many are not realistic representations so cannot accurately be attributed to a specific piece of artillery. As with their real counterparts on the battlefields of France, models of shells were produced in prolific quantities. Some examples by Arcadian and Grafton were inscribed 'Jack Johnson', the nickname given to the actual shell by the British to describe the impact. The name was taken from the world heavyweight boxing champion of the same name.

Military Transport – Over fifty different models of tanks are known, along with approximately thirty-three aeroplanes and seventy-five ships of which just over forty bear the name of ships of the fleet.

Made by numerous china manufacturers from the better known such as Carlton, to the relatively obscure companies like Pearl Arms and Florentine, the difference in each factory's model was in size rather than design. In general, the sizes would range from the largest at 180mm (Arcadian Tank) down to the smallest at 80mm (Carlton 'Crème-de-Menthe' Tank).

A number of the same models can be found featuring the 'Flags of the Allies' and the popular motto of the day 'United We Stand'.

(Author's Collection)

J E Beales Postcard

During the war years, Bournemouth still enjoyed a steady stream of holiday makers, and as one would expect, there were a number of retail outlets where it would have been possible to purchase a 'war/holiday' souvenir. On most pieces, the town's coat of arms is the standard navy/yellow colourway, but occasionally pieces can be found with an addition of pale blue to the standard. Models of artillery shells would have resonated amongst local folk, as in July 1915 several local companies turned their production lines over to the making of munitions. Engineering firms such as,

Edwards and Co. were awarded contracts to produce eighteen pounder shells and at the end of the war it was reported that Bournemouth Motor Syndicate had produced over 250,000 shells 'the greatest number made by any one firm in the West of England'.

From items in the author's own collection, it would appear that there were three main department stores in the town who stocked crested military china; J E Harrison, Commercial Road, Bournemouth (Hand Grenade & Torpedo Boat Destroyer); G Hill & Son, 62 Commercial Road, Bournemouth (British Military Helmet); J E Beales, Bournemouth (Carlton Bi-plane).

Although originally sold as cheap trinkets for the holiday maker, rarer items of crested china now command high prices, as these simple mementos of a bygone age have now become today's sought-after item of WW1 memorabilia. Perhaps Goss China may have had the benefit of foresight in their somewhat pretentious statement in the *Pottery Gazette* 2 April 1917:

'Goss china upholds the time-honoured association of ceramics with topical and historical events as a means of establishing a permanent and abiding memory. Pottery is to archaeology what fossils are to geology'

04 Army Prayer Book and Card

Billeting: Army Life: Life in the Town: Religion: Local Lives

Almost from the outbreak of the First World War, Bournemouth was one of many towns that earned the name garrison town, due to the high number of infantry regiments from all parts of the country that were billeted in private homes. Accommodation had to be found in the early months for over 10,000 men and by November 1914 the number had increased to approximately 16,000. Homes were found in areas away from the centre of town; Moordown, Winton, Boscombe and Pokesdown being some of the first selected to provide beds for men from regiments that included:

Royal Field Artillery
Royal Garrison Artillery
The Loyal North Lancashire Regiment
Royal Welsh Fusiliers

Most households welcomed this opportunity to bring some much-needed additional income into the home. The standard rate laid down by the War Office was 3d per man per night, with meals provided at extra cost. The larger boarding houses in the centre of town felt aggrieved that they were not given the same opportunity. However, no doubt there were a few matriarchs, who, as in other towns, claimed they had sick children in the house or refused to answer the knock on the door. The only accepted reason for refusing a billeting request was if there were no males in residence.

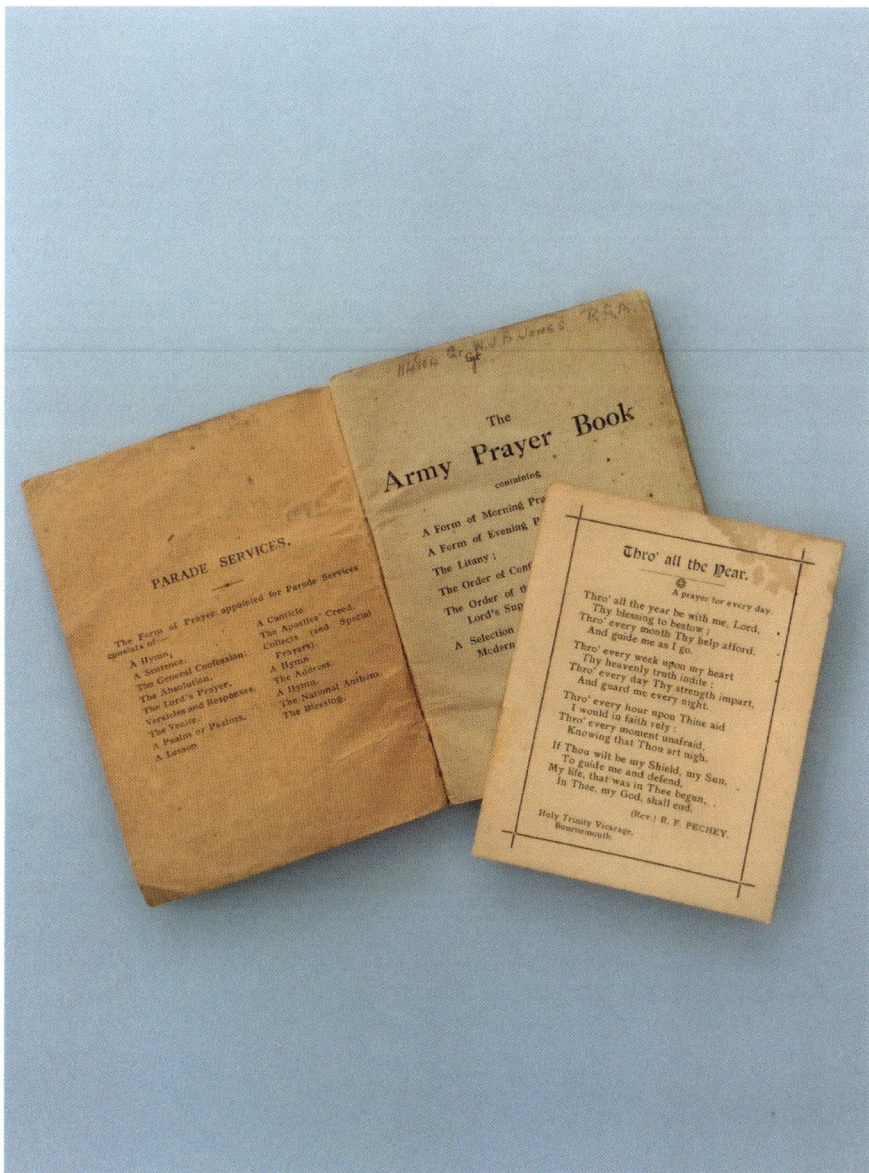

In most cases, two or three men were assigned to a home, generating a not inconsiderable sum per week to the struggling family. The *Bournemouth Graphic* of September 1914 makes light of the situation by reporting somewhat tongue in cheek of an incident when on being questioned by an officer, a lady on the West Cliff is understood to have said that the number of family residing at the house was five, but the canary had since died! Although the number of homes being allocated soldiers was considerable, it was by no means certain that the offer of residence would be accepted, many hundreds had their applications refused.

Many strong bonds of friendship were formed between the mother of the family and their guests, not based on the remuneration that was received. Young soldiers away from home for the first time grew genuinely attached to their 'billet mother', a feeling that without doubt was reciprocated. The family of Private Ernest Kiveal back home in Manchester would have the pain of sending their lad off to war eased by knowing he was being taken care of in a family home. When Ernest left for training at a camp in Romsey he sent back 'A Soldier's letter to his Billet Mother' Mrs Thorne, 199 Stewart Road, Bournemouth in May 1915 on which he wrote:

'Dear Ma, just a line to let you know that camp is not as good for feeding as your billet. I am going home at the weekend for six days so I will have a good time it will beat everything.
One of your lodgers Ernest' (sic)

Sadly, research shows that Private Ernest Kiveal 14357, 8th Kings Own (Royal Lancashire Regiment), son of Michael & Sarah, was killed in action on 16 August 1916 aged 23. He is commemorated on the Thiepval Memorial.

Private Charles Edward Miller, remembered in the Bournemouth Book of Remembrance, also served in the Kings Own (Royal Lancashire) Regiment, and was killed at the Battle of the Somme on 3 July 1916, he is also listed on the Thiepval Memorial.

Billet Memories.

A Soldier's Letter to his " Billet Mother."

YOU mothered us well in the cold winter months,
    When mud and the rain were supreme ;
And we were sorry when the time came for us to go,
    To the Camp where the hills are so green.
We know we were a " handful " at times,
    But *you* never made any fuss ;
The Clerk of the Weather was mostly to blame,
    Your only thoughts were of " *us.*"
We've oft seen it advertised a " Home from Home,"
    Well that our old billet just fits ;
And as for the " grub " and the cooking, dear Ma,
    We all must confess 'twas just " *it.*"
" Home Comforts " are now few and far between,
    For we're shortly going over the sea ;
But your old Billet Boys will be doing their " *bit,*"
    En route to " Berlin on the *Spree.*"
Thoughts of *YOU* and *YOURS* are with us,
    Whether we're at work or play ;
" KIND REMEMBRANCE " to all our old friends,
    Of the Billet down.............way.

From *E Kiveal*   At *Romsey*

COPYRIGHT.

(Author's Collection)

Private Ernest Kiveal's Postcard to his 'Billet Mother'

The influx of men into the town, both those in home billets and those under canvas in camps at Iford and Tuckton caused not insignificant problems for Bournemouth. Besides requiring space enough for drills and training, in order that they did not become a disruptive presence they needed recreational facilities, entertainment and somewhere to spend their free time. 'Many Church halls were utilised and donations of cards, chess sets, games, magazines and newspapers were requested.' (M A Edgington). In addition to Church halls being used as recreational venues, YMCA huts were erected across the town to meet the growing demand. By 1916, eight huts were providing refreshment and facilities for the men, the Kennedy Memorial YMCA hut being moved from its original site to the square.

Some of the troops billeted in Moordown during the first winter of the war were the Welsh Fusiliers and Borderers, who were only too pleased to escape the cold and wet that marked the winter of 1914-15, and find a warm fire and a comfortable bed. A consequence of the welcome given in Moordown was noted by the Reverend Bloomfield who wrote in the history of St John's Church, 'A number of the survivors formed links with our Parish which eventually led to a number, we believe, of happy marriages with Moordown girls.'

While the available theatre and cinema entertainment would have found favour with the troops before their departure overseas, a high proportion of the men would also have sought comfort and spiritual guidance in any of the town's churches. Most faith groups supported the war, preaching sermons justifying the cause and offering up prayers for specific regiments and individual fighting men. The Rev. J Hutton of Richmond Hill Congregational Church had no doubt that, 'the battle is not ours but God's' when he preached his sermon on the righteousness of the cause in September 1914. For those at home, religious faith had been the mainstay of everyday life and totally aligned with patriotism whatever the denomination. However, for those in the trenches, religion was a curious mix of faith and superstition. Chaplains, and occasionally rabbis were assigned to each unit; the Christian padres offering communion and prayers for the dying when required. Many battle-hardened soldiers ensured they carried their small bible, containing Lord Robert's message:

'I ask you to put your trust in God. He will watch over you and strengthen you. You will find in this little Book guidance when you are in health, comfort when you are in sickness and strength when you are in adversity'
25 August 1914.

The church of their faith would also supply a departing soldier with religious tracts and images, designed to bring comfort and a degree of luck. The destruction of churches and religious icons took on a special significance for those on the battlefield. Every soldier firmly believed the superstition that if the Golden Virgin on top of the basilica in Albert (France) fell then the war would be over. Angels comforting the dying or watching over the men were popular images of the day, confirming that right and God were on the side of the British.

The Holy Trinity Church in Old Christchurch Road was one of the many local churches which offered spiritual comfort to the men billeted in the town before they set off into the unknown. The prayer card issued by the Rev. R F Pechey would have resonated with a young soldier facing his first battle, imparting the message that the Lord would strengthen, guard and defend him. Those of strong religious belief would certainly have felt that reciting this prayer on the Western Front would protect them through the onslaught. The small Army Prayer Book is a pared down version of the book of common prayer containing details of the order for 'Parades Services', Psalms, Hymns and on the end page – the National Anthem. 1,5000,000 of these prayer books were printed, and the copy pictured here, belonging to Gunner Sergeant W J Jones, is numbered 6/16 indicating its year of print as 1916. Research has identified Gunner Sergeant Jones, to be Warriet James Brown Jones 114804, RGA who was born in Mathry, Wales in 1898 and who at some point in his army life was billeted in

Bournemouth. Warriet's medal index card shows that by the end of the war his rank was that of Bombardier. In 1925 he married his first wife Hilda, and in 1939 he and Hilda were living in Wembley (London), where he worked as an export buyer. Warriet James Brown Jones died in October 1987, approximately seventy years since as a young Gunner Sergeant in the RGA he found a welcome in the town of Bournemouth and certainly spiritual comfort at the Holy Trinity Church.

'Thoughts of YOU and YOURS are with us, Whether we're at work or play; Kind Remembrance to all our friends, Of the Billet down *Bournemouth* way'

From E Kiveal

05 Military Cigarette Silk

Lance-Corporal Cecil Reginald Noble

Advertising: Army Life: Battle of Neuve Chapelle: Military Decorations: Local Lives

Smoking for the Tommies of WW1 was considered by most Colonels in charge of the troops to be a necessity rather than a luxury. The morale boosting effects, together with the medicinal properties for the men following combat and bombardment were never underestimated. According to official estimates, over 96 per cent of British soldiers at the start of 1915 were smokers, and those who had not been smokers at the start of the war were smoking regularly by the end of it. Smoking was actively encouraged amongst the men: farewell gifts of tobacco on departure for the front; cigarettes issued along with the daily rations; the common practice of using cigarettes as currency, all combined to ensure the manufacturers of tobacco products fought hard for their share of the market. The popularity of cigarette smoking both at home and overseas during WW1 soon replaced that of pipe smoking which had previously been the most popular method of smoking by the military. During 1915 British soldiers and sailors smoked around 1000 tons of cigarettes.

Charities, such as the YMCA and the Red Cross, played their part in ensuring the steady supply of cigarettes to the troops fighting on all fronts, not least by holding regular fund-raising events. 'Smokes for the Troops' was a popular slogan aimed at the patriotic spirit of those at home wanting to do their bit for the boys of the

The Late Corpl. CECIL. R. NOBLE.

THE RIFLE BRIGADE.
(The Prince Consorts Own).

army and navy. To make it easier for the public to send cigarettes and tobacco to members of the BEF, the Post Office allowed them to be mailed at letter postal rate instead of parcel rate.

(Author's Collection)

Cigarette Advertising Postcard

The cigarette companies lost no time in promoting their products and encouraging smoking by means of clever advertising which captured the spirit of the day. Not only did postcards of the war years feature the smiling British Tommy enjoying his much needed 'fag', but large adverts for all the main cigarette brands were published in every national newspaper. One brand, Con Amore, produced a range of 200 regimental cigarettes, with the crest of the regiment printed neatly onto the cigarette itself. Their newspaper adverts exhorted the public to 'send a box to your Fighting Friend that would be a compliment to his regiment as well as a mark of remembrance and cheer'. The choice of the name Con Amore with its meaning of 'with love or devotion' and its slogan 'In Trench, Mess, Billet or Shipboard every smoke will remind him of you – the giver' was a marketing strategy aimed at the sweetheart left at home and guaranteed the makers a share of the expanding market.

The practice of giving away cards inside packets of cigarettes was a sales ploy that had started in 1902, but which gathered momentum during the First World War as every cigarette manufacturer sought to entice new custom. Original subjects of animals, flowers, and cars gave way to military subjects with the outbreak of war, children continuing to eagerly collect the new military cards. Black Cat cigarettes produced sets of cards based on the wartime cartoons of Louis Raemaekers, and D & H O Wills a set of fifty Military Motors. Both sets were sought after by young collectors. Although most companies stuck to small card inserts, others such as BDV employed Godfrey Phillips to produce images on printed or woven satin. These military silks, with regimental crests, flags and eventually VC winners proved popular with not only male smokers, but with the burgeoning female market whose buying power brought about by the increase in women workers, was exploited fully by the tobacco companies. Women were eager to obtain the silks found inside the cigarette packets, some of which also included instructions for making household items such as quilts from the colourful pieces of fabric. The production of the 'silk' cigarette card had its heyday in the years of the First World War, and by 1922 the practice of cigarette silks had all but gone.

Lance-Corporal Cecil Reginald Noble VC, known in his family as Tommy, was born in Tower Road, Bournemouth on 4 June 1891 to Frederick, a decorator, and Hannah. Although two further sons were born, only his sister Florence survived infancy. In 1901 the family were living in Lincoln Avenue, but by 1911 they had moved to Holdenhurst Road, Bournemouth. Cecil was educated at St Clement's School in the town and then the Art & Technical School. By the end of WW1, the family had moved again to 'Ferndean' 172 Capstone Road. On 31 March 1910, 'Tommy' enlisted in the Rifle Brigade (The Prince Consort's Own) at the age of 19. He was assigned the regimental number 3697, and after an initial posting with the 2nd Battalion to India in November 1911, sailed back to Liverpool in September 1914 after the outbreak of the war. As part of C Company, 'Tommy' landed in France on 7 November and was appointed an Acting Corporal on the 23 of the same month.

On 11 March 1915, at Neuve Chapelle (France), the 2nd Battalion had spent the day in the trenches awaiting orders to advance on the German defences. Orders were finally received for an attack to commence at 07.30 hrs the following morning. After the proposed attack was delayed twice, and following a 30-minute artillery bombardment, the British attack finally got under way at 12.30 hrs. A & B Company left their trench for the assault on the enemy's line, but they were met with a hail of fire. Many men fell, and in the face of such opposition the attack was halted. At 16.00 hrs a second attack was ordered for 17.15 hrs which was 'to be pressed home at any cost'. Lance-Corporal Noble and C Company, along with the men of D Company were ordered forward. C Company came under intense machine gun fire and D Company had their way forward blocked by uncut wire. This wire needed to be cut and instead of picking men at random for this most perilous task, CSM Harry Daniels asked his friend Corporal Noble to accompany him. Armed with wire cutters the two men managed to cover the few yards to the wire under heavy machine gun fire and lying on their backs began to cut first the lower strands. They then gradually worked their way up unscathed, until on their knees, they began to tackle the highest part of the wire. Daniels was the first to be hit in the thigh, following which Cecil Noble was hit in the chest.

Lance-Corporal Cecil 'Tommy' Noble died of his wounds the following day aged 23 and is buried in Longuenesse Souvenir Cemetery. Notice of his VC commendation appeared in *The London Gazette* of the 28 April 1915:

'His Majesty the KING has been graciously pleased to approve the grant of the Victoria Cross to the undermentioned Warrant Office, non-commissioned officer, and men for their conspicuous acts of bravery and devotion to duty whilst serving with the Expeditionary Force.'

Hannah Noble was presented with her son's VC by the King at Buckingham Palace on 29 November 1916. He was also awarded the 1914 Star with Mons clasp, British War Medal and Victory Medal. Until 2015 in his home town of Bournemouth, Lance-Corporal Cecil Noble had been remembered on a bronze memorial plaque in St Clement's School, a blue plaque in Capstone Road, and by the naming of a road, Noble Close. At the centenary of his death, the town was presented with a commemorative paving stone by the government, which was laid by the War Memorial and unveiled in a special ceremony attended by the author on Thursday 12 March 2015.

On 1 October 2018, a further paving stone was unveiled commemorating the second of the two VC winners to be born in the town, Sergeant Frederick Charles Riggs of the York and Lancaster Regiment. Coincidently, Sergeant Riggs lived in Capstone Road, where his blue plaque is also sited.

'The best chum I've ever had, the bravest man I've ever known'

Harry Daniels' tribute to 'Tommy' Noble

(Author's Collection)

Corporal Noble Paving Slab

06 Bournemouth Crested Ship & Tank

Royal Navy: Fundraising: Tank Development: WW1 Souvenirs: Crested China: Local Lives

Very little is said about the sailors from Bournemouth who served in the Royal and Merchant Navy during WW1, and while too often those who were killed in the infantry are remembered, the same cannot be said about the sailors who lost their lives. The names of at least eighty-one sailors who classed Bournemouth as their home are remembered for the most part on either the Portsmouth or Plymouth Naval Memorials. Twenty-four of those were killed during The Battle of Jutland on 31 May 1916, and a further four were lost with Lord Kitchener when the HMS Hampshire struck a mine on 5 June 1916. The death of Lord Kitchener and the loss of the men on board was keenly felt in the town. Approximately 5,000 people turned out in the cold and wet to attend a memorial concert on the pier given by the Municipal Orchestra, the Last Post being played by men of the 4th Volunteer Battalion, Hampshire Regiment. When, on 13 June, a service was held at St Paul's, households drew their curtains, shops closed and the bells of St Peter's tolled.

The sailors of Bournemouth may not have received the same centenary commemorations as their counterparts in the infantry, but certainly during the war years the part the Royal Navy played in defending Great Britain was acknowledged. In 1914, Britain was still the world's greatest naval and maritime power, but as the war progressed this position of strength was weakened by the threat posed to its fleets by the German High Seas Fleet and their U-Boats. Britain's naval and maritime fleets had to be maintained in order to

safeguard the nation's security. A letter from the Board of Trade to the Cabinet warned:

'the shortage of shipping will place this country in more serious peril than can any calamity short of the defeat of the Navy.'

Bournemouth was determined to do its bit in ensuring that the ships of the Royal Navy continued to defend Britain's shores. Early in 1918 a major fundraising week took place with the aim of raising £150,000 in war bonds to purchase a destroyer for the Royal Navy. The square was decorated with flags and streamers, with one hoarding plastered with an image of the 'HMS Bournemouth' destroyer under full steam. A tramcar fitted inside as a bank, the outside decorated with 'Buy War Bonds' placards, received donations and issued the bonds. The final sum achieved, £252,892, enough to buy a heavy gunboat, far exceeded all expectations.

Virtually all manufacturers of military ceramics included one or more models of warships in their range. Today it is possible to find both named and unnamed replica ships of the First World War, but most are unrealistic in their design. Carlton Ware produced ten different models, using fifteen of the names of ships found in the fleet. The HMS Queen Elizabeth, then a new class of ship and described as 'the finest battleship ever' was Admiral of the Fleet David Beatty's flagship and therefore well known amongst the public. As such it was popular amongst the buying public and five different manufacturers produced models to meet the demand. Arcadian China, one of the largest producers of crested military china, unusually made only five naval models: three warships in different sizes, a torpedo destroyer and a model of a trawler. The quantity produced by the Arcadian China company make them one of the more frequently found pieces for today's collector.

The introduction of the tank into the British war arsenal captured the imagination and curiosity of the nation when they first appeared in the *Daily Mirror* on 22 November 1916. Although the early Mark 1 Tank, with its two large rearward steering wheels had been seen on the battlefield for the first time in September 1916, the British public had not been allowed to see pictures of these 'polychromatic toads'. These new weapons of war were considered 'hush hush' until their publication in the press. Fascination with this monstrous creation, exciting new technology to the people of an Edwardian era, further increased with the construction of the Mark IV tank in April 1917, the first of its type to have no steering wheels.

Following the success of the tank at the Battle of Cambrai in November 1917, tanks toured towns and cities during the winter months as part of the War Bonds 'Tank Bank' campaign. For the towns visited this was a momentous event, young and old excitedly joined the crowds viewing this strange 'land ship'. The tank would stay for a week at a time, advertising the sale of war bonds. War Savings Certificates could be bought for fifteen shillings and six pence, raising millions of pounds for the war effort. After the war, these same certificates could be redeemed for £1 each.

(Author's Collection)

Tank Bank Postcard

Bournemouth was not one of the towns granted the privilege of a visit from a tank. This caused a certain amount of dissatisfaction which was taken up by the *Bournemouth Guardian* whose editor gave voice to the complaints:

' Other towns have guns presented to them in some sort of semi-recognition...we have not even had the visit of a real tank...yet if any town can claim to have done well, both in sending men in proportion to its adult population to the front or in finding money to carry out the war, Bournemouth has a very high record.'

(Author's Collection)

Drawing from small sketch book

Having a tank in your town for a week had its disadvantages, as the Council would discover when they were finally offered a tank visit. On being informed that host sites would be responsible for its security and maintenance – the Council swiftly declined the offer. Tanks would eventually be seen in Bournemouth in December 1918. During Victory Bond Week, six tanks processed from the Central Station to the square, where the Mayor then gave a speech from the top of one.

Certainly, of all the crested china pieces produced it was the armoured cars and tanks that proved most popular. Thirty different model tanks were produced by a variety of potteries. The first models appeared weeks after their first use on the Somme, but the modellers had to rely on written descriptions as no photos had yet been made available. Models still found today come in various sizes and by different manufacturers, in both the two wheeled Mark 1 and unwheeled Mark IV versions. The Arcadian 320mm Mark IV is considered to be a shop display model due to its size. Following on from the success of the 'Tank Bank' campaign, most china companies produced their own scaled down savings Tank Bank, although the Shelley model had a slot so thin it would only take notes or very thin coins. The drawback to these as savings banks was that they had to be smashed to get the money out.

At least six Bournemouth men, killed during the First World War, had transferred from regular regiments to the newly created Tank Corps. One who survived the war was Harold George Head, an old boy from Bournemouth School who had enlisted in the Hampshire Cyclists Regiment, then transferred to the heavy section of the Machine Gun Corps where he was placed in charge of a Tank. In October 1918, his tank was supporting the infantry to the North of Flers-Courcelette, and in doing so took out a German machine gun and destroyed the trench lines. Harold Head was awarded the MC.

'You have heard of the wonderful tanks, there are legends about them in plenty'

A A Milne

07 Field Service Postcards

Private J Garwood to Mrs L Hayman

Army Postal Service: Censorship: Army Life: Faith & Religion: Local Lives

Field service postcards (Army Form A2042) were introduced early into WW1 in an attempt to overcome the issue of censorship in mail sent from the Front. The need to maintain secrecy and ensure no useful information fell into the hands of the enemy resulted in every piece of post that was sent back to England having first to pass through the hands of the unit censor. It was also felt that by monitoring the letters and postcards sent home, the morale of the men could be ascertained, especially important after major battles and during periods of harsh living conditions. Censoring the mail was a time-consuming job for the junior officers of the unit. An unsealed letter or postcard when handed in, would be read and countersigned by the young officer before being passed to the officer in charge of the censor stamp. Any offending word or sentence would be crossed out, usually with a blue pencil, and any postcards featuring a picture of a village or town would have the place name scratched through with a sharp instrument.

Six different shapes of censor stamp were used on mail from the western front at different periods of the war, and although usually red ink was used other colours are known to exist.

At the outbreak of war: CM1 Circular
November 1914: CM2 Square

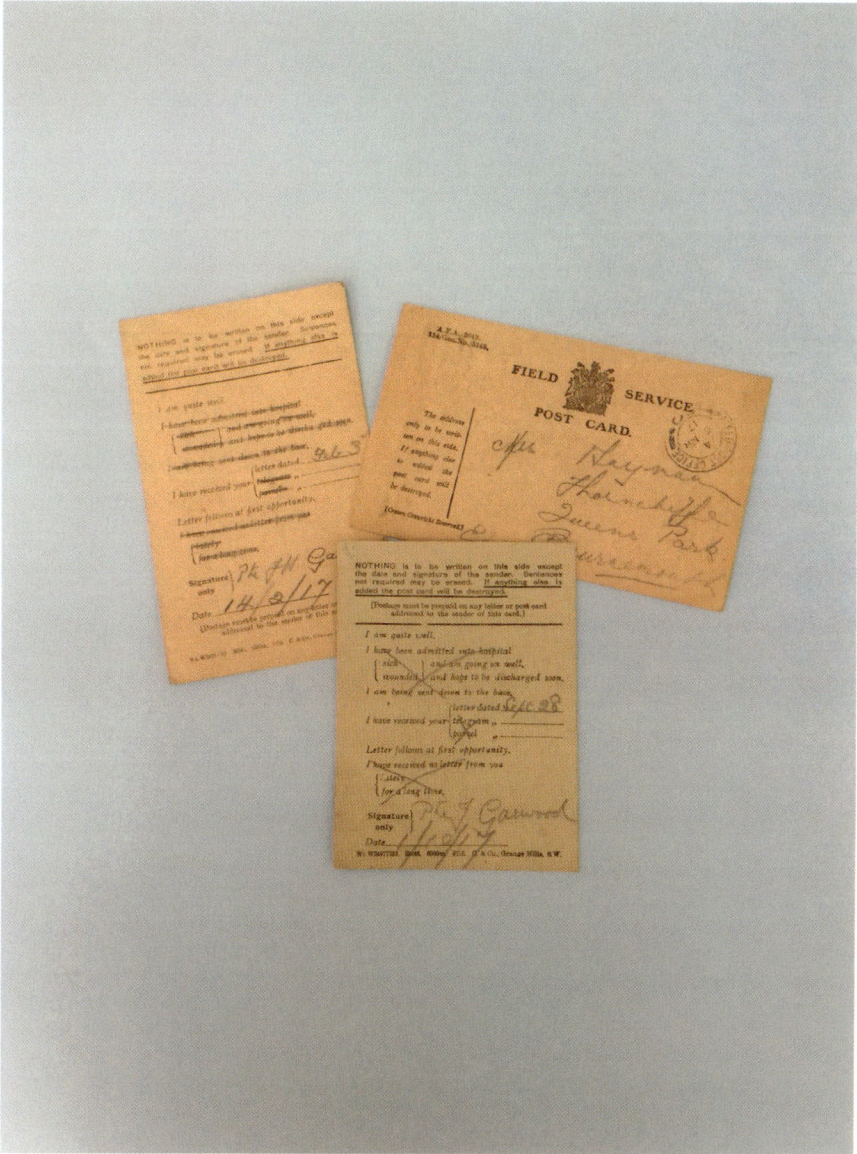

April 1915: CM3 Triangle
January 1916: CM4 Hexagonal
November 1916: CM5 Oval
A final version appeared in October 1917: CM6 Rectangle.

Therefore, the introduction of Field Service Postcards was seen as an innovative way to tackle the problem of censorship. Each soldier would be issued with standard beige coloured postcards that were pre-printed with a series of innocuous phrases that could be either deleted or retained. Space was left on the postcard for only the insertion of the date on which post had been received by the soldier, their signature, and the date sent. Families waiting for news anxiously at home received a modicum of comfort from standard phrases such as 'I am quite well' or 'Letter follows at first opportunity', however they actually learned little of how their loved one was really feeling, or the conditions they were enduring.

The first Field Service Postcards carried an impressed penny stamp on the address side, but after the introduction of free postage for serving troops in all the areas of conflict this was removed. Alongside the address was a warning that the card would be destroyed if anything other than the address was written. By removing the need to pass through the hands of the censor, these basic postcards were processed through the postal system faster than standard mail, leading to their nick name 'whizz-bangs'. Such was their popularity that although initially rationed to the men at the rate of two per week, they were later issued on demand during periods of heavy fighting. By the autumn of 1917, when Private Garwood sent the final postcard pictured, 285,000 items of mail had been sent by the British Expeditionary Force, as a consequence the Field Service Postcard (FSP) was reduced in size due to paper shortages.

Although the intention of the FSP was to limit the flow of information to the civilian population back home, one member of the 'Richmond Sixteen', a group of conscientious objectors sent to France as an example and subsequently sentenced to death for refusing to obey a direct order, managed to defy authorities when allowed to send an FSP. By deleting some of each phrase, while retaining certain letters, he was able to construct a secret message hidden in the card informing those in England as to their fate. Such was the public outcry, that the sentence was commuted to life which would be served in an English prison.

Following on from the success of the Field Service Postcard, in March 1915 special green envelopes were issued to the troops for their longer letters home. Like the postcards, the contents of these green envelopes would not be censored if the declaration certificate on the reverse had been signed - 'I certify on my honour that the contents of the envelope refer to nothing but private and family matters.' Known as 'honour envelopes' they proved very popular with the men, but inevitably this promise was occasionally contravened, and the envelopes would contain banned information regarding casualty numbers and battle plans. In 1916 a second version of the green envelope with the certification on the front making inspection easier, was produced. However, as with the postcards the popularity of the envelopes led to a shortage of green paper and they were replaced with buff envelopes with green printing.

In 1917 Private J H Garwood was making use of his allocation of Field Service Postcards in order to correspond with Mrs L Hayman of 'Thorncliffe' Queens Park, Bournemouth. Research into determining details about Private J H Garwood has not been successful. The cards on initial inspection give very little away, as was their intention. Checking the records for soldiers of that name who died during the war, only one, J E Garwood, was killed after the 1 October 1917 (date of postcard), therefore it can be assumed that he survived. The only additional information gleaned from the cards, comes from the post mark or 'cancelling'. The postcards are sent from a Field Post Office, small mobile units attached to a brigade or division, often set up in a ruined chateau or barn, which then moved with the army when it received fresh orders. Those sent by Private Garwood in February and March 1917 have the code number 60 at the bottom of the cancellation mark which indicates that at that time he was serving with the 60th Brigade. The 60th Brigade, part of 'Kitchener's Army', were assigned to the 20th (Light) Division on the Western Front. At the beginning of January 1917, the Division had returned to the Front, two and a half miles south of Le Transloy, where they remained, holding the line and defending against German attacks until they were relieved at the end of the month. The German army began to retreat from the line in front of the 20th Division on 17 March. From 16 August 1917, the 60th Brigade were attacking towards and around the town of Langemarck as part of the Third Battle of Ypres. Records show that on 1 October 1917, the 20th Division 'less the artillery' decamped for Bapaume. Private Garwood's later card, dated coincidentally 1/10/17, now bears a cancellation mark giving the code number 108, for the 108th Brigade, part of the 36th (Ulster) Division. Given that the 36th Division were also in the area of Langemarck at the same time as the 20th Division, it would be reasonable to speculate that Private J Garwood was serving in the artillery, and as such did not leave for Bapaume with the rest of the 60th Brigade but was transferred to the 108th. A further contributing factor to this speculation is the billeting of artillery troops in Bournemouth where Private Garwood in all likelihood met the recipient of the cards – Mrs L. Hayman.

Lilian Emma Hayman, born in Bristol in 1865, was the wife of William Speed Hayman, Doctor of Medicine. They had 2 children, daughter Annie Morwenna and son William Rollo Lenden. In 1911, the family were living in Brighton, but by the outbreak of the First World War, they had moved again to Queens Park, Bournemouth, where William Rollo attended first Wychwood Preparatory School and then Sherbourne School. Lilian was devoted to her family and her life in the church and both in Brighton and Bournemouth she ran Bible classes which she continued to offer to the young men living and billeted in the town. Lilian encouraged them to consider the teachings of the Bible and how they applied to the war. She referred to these young soldiers and sailors as 'her boys' and when they were sent overseas would write to them all regularly giving them spiritual comfort and hope in the darkest of days.

Private Garwood was not alone in corresponding with his Bible school teacher. In January 1915, one of her 'boys' serving in the navy wrote to her, 'Your old Bible class, dear Teacher is making history...... they are lining up, going forth nobly to fight'. Lilian Hayman was loved and respected not only by the young men who had spent time in her home both before and after the war, but by all who knew her at her church (St Mary the Virgin), and in the community. Mrs Hayman continued her Bible classes right up until her death in 1944 aged 80. We may not be able to establish the identity or service details of Private J H Garwood, but we do know that his life was touched and comforted by Bournemouth resident Mrs L Hayman.

'Generations of 'her lads' owe more than they can ever express in words'

Obituary – St Mary the Virgin Parish Newsletter

S. MARY THE VIRGIN. SPRINGBOURNE. IN 1921.

(Courtesy of Alwyn Ladell)

St Mary the Virgin Church Postcard

08 Wooden Bookends

Disabled Soldiers & Sailors: Rehabilitation: Local Lives

The villa 'Grata Quies' (29 Western Avenue, Branksome) was originally lent to Poole by its owner as a home for Belgian refugees, but opened in November 1914 as an auxiliary hospital for wounded Belgian soldiers. In order that these recuperating men could make a small living, Miss Hilda Amy Smith was employed to teach them how to make and paint toys which would then be sold locally. When the Belgians left in November 1915, the British wounded soldiers who were sent to 'Grata Quies' did not want to continue the work, so a new home was found for the 'workshop' at Tachbrook, a council owned property in Bath Road, next to the Belle Vue Hotel which had also been earmarked as a home for Belgian refugees back in 1914.

The Tachbrook Toy Factory, with Miss Smith still at the helm, opened in February 1916, offering employment to any remaining Belgians and possibly any British soldiers discharged as unfit. The *Bournemouth Graphic* of April 1918 refers to Tachbrook as 'The Tachbrook Belgian Toy Hospital', with the by-line 'Helping Belgium to Help Herself,' reference to the scheme's aim of being self-supporting. The working day for the 'employees' was from 9.30am until 4pm, payment for which was weekly according to ability. The community workshop at Tachbrook proved very successful and was welcomed locally by the town's residents who followed its development and the increasing attention the toyshop was attracting with interest. The range of toys produced by the

enthusiastic workforce, who made not only those of traditional designs, but those to their own original specification grew steadily, their 'Nursery Rhyme' range proving most popular.

(Bournemouth Graphic)

Tachbrook Toy Advertisement

At the 'Wounded Warriors Exhibition' in London, 1917, toys made at Tachbrook and available for sale, formed part of the exhibition of handicrafts made by injured soldiers. Such was the appreciation of the quality of work produced by the men of

Tachbrook, that a complete set of toys was ordered by an American doctor to be sent to the USA as examples of what could be achieved by the American wounded. Amongst the number of large orders received, The Tachbrook Toy Company received Royal recognition when Queen Mary and Queen Alexandra purchased items from the stand.

Back in Bournemouth, the *Graphic* reported that not only was the toy factory in Bath Road becoming something of a 'magical' tourist attraction, but 'an interesting feature of the workshops is the Saturday crowd of children of all ages, who each do their 'little bit' in learning to make toys.' However prolific the output of Tachbrook undoubtably was, the author has yet to see a toy item made at the factory.

The need to provide training and employment for soldiers disabled during the war was recognised as the war drew to a close. What had been achieved by the men at Tachbrook was an example of how, with the right training, men could still provide for their families when unable to resume their pre-war occupations. Before the cessation of hostilities, the Municipal College in Bournemouth began classes in fancy leather work for wounded ex-servicemen, leading to the opening of a factory at the corner of Spring Road which employed those trained at the college to make handbags, writing cases etc. This project proved such a success that the Ministry of Pensions advised extending the training classes to include other practical skills like book binding and cabinet making.

At the end of the war, the Tachbrook Toy Factory was initially allowed to continue in its present home, but employing disabled British soldiers to replace the Belgians who were returning home. However, the site had for some time been procured for building the Pavilion that we know today, so an alternative site for what would now be called the Disabled Soldiers and Sailors Workshops was found in Peter's Hill, Wimborne Road, Winton. Miss Hilda Smith, the original tutor at Tachbrook back in 1916, relocated with the meagre assets of the factory to an old army hut on the site of what had been the Winton National Kitchen during the war years. The workshop, in its new home, retained its disabled ex-soldier workforce and with Miss Smith, working unpaid alongside 'her men', continued to grow until eventually new premises were built on the same site in 1929. In the New Year's honours list of 1939, Miss Smith was awarded the MBE by George V in recognition of her work which she continued to do right through WW2, and up until a few months before her death in 1959.

'To the men she is a mother, a nurse, a psychiatrist, a friend and a confidant'

Mayor of Bournemouth Cllr W J Whitelock

09 WW1 Sweetheart Brooches

Love Tokens: Remembrance: Manufacturing

After the declaration of war on 4 August 1914, and following the proclamation mobilising territorial forces, the members of the local units began reporting to their headquarters. Large crowds turned out to cheer the 7th Battalion, Hampshire Regiment as they reported for duty. This was the beginning of the Bournemouth men leaving their homes and loved ones and preparing for combat.

By 26 August, the rush to volunteer saw about 350 local lads join the regular forces, keen not to miss out on the greatest 'adventure' of their lives and to fight for 'King and Country'. Bournemouth became a garrison town almost from the day war was declared, and 10-12,000 men from all parts of England were billeted across the town, many forming friendships with their billet 'mother' and the local girls before being sent overseas to fight. By early 1915, those remaining at home had realised that the war, meant to be 'over by Christmas', was stretching into another long year, and the casualty lists published in the local newspapers were growing ever longer. The young men who had so excitedly joined the frenzy to enlist now knew what awaited them overseas. They left for training, followed by shipment to the areas of fighting, never knowing whether they would see their mothers, wives or sweethearts again. In their desire to leave their loved one a token of affection or remembrance, and symbolic of the emotional connection between giver and wearer, the 'sweetheart brooch' became a popular parting gift.

The giving of military jewellery as a love token, had been

around since the late 1800s, and by the time of the Boer war, jewellers had been asked to solder a pin onto the back of a regimental badge to make it into a brooch for a lady. Jewellery manufacturers soon realised the commercial potential of these emotive items and began to produce their own versions that ranged from the simplest, made from base metal with no more than a safety pin attachment, through to finer versions made from gold, sometimes studded with jewels. Originally called Military or Regimental Badge Brooches, they featured the service, regimental or home town crest of the soldier, the simpler ones on a background of mother of pearl – a marriage of military and romance.

(Author's Collection)

Postcard of young lady wearing Sweetheart Brooch

As demand and popularity grew, manufacturers produced an ever-increasing range of styles and designs which now result in them becoming a popular item for modern-day collectors who have now adopted the name 'Sweetheart Brooch' as a standard term. Rifles, wishbones, entwined hearts and anchors are just some of the styles that originated during the First World War, along with the more traditional regimental crest, all of which were worn with pride for the hero gone to war. It is also true that the wearing of a brooch signified that a young lady was 'taken', thereby a warning to other young men.

While the gold, silver and jewelled versions found favour with the officer ranks, the affordability of the cheaper versions ensured that all departing 'Tommies' could purchase a token for their sweetheart, mother, or friend. It is often these particular brooches that are more evocative of the generation decimated by First World War. In her book *Military Sweetheart Jewellery* Pamela Caunt states that, 'in 1917 a dozen silver 'sweethearts' wholesaled for one pound, a gold one sold for fourteen shillings and a full gross of gilt badges cost a mere three pounds and twelve shillings'.

Along with the more traditional sweetheart brooches, the term has evolved to cover two further types of brooch:

1   Western Front souvenir brooches. To meet the demand for souvenirs, French manufacturers produced base metal brooches, featuring the name of the town or battlefield in gilded letters. Places names such as Arras, Somme, Ypres were snapped up by both British and German troops during the war, and by battlefield tourists post-war.

2   Trench Art brooches. Often considered to be of greater sentimental value than the shop bought ones to the wearer, due to being fashioned from cast offs found by the soldier and handmade. Brooches fashioned from spent bullets, tunic buttons or coins are often found.

Those seen in the main photo are:

Centre – Royal Engineers Sweetheart Brooch on original card
Top Left – White metal brooch inscribed 'Ypres'
Top Right – Gilt base metal brooch inscribed 'Somme'
Bottom Right – Mother-of-Pearl 'Bournemouth' Sweetheart Brooch
Bottom Left – Rifle Brigade Sweetheart Brooch

Although still made during the Second World War, more modern designs began to replace the mother of pearl, or tortoise shell variety, and eventually the popularity of the Sweetheart Brooch began to decline. However, today these simple brooches encapsulate the sentiment of the time, when pride, duty, comradeship and honour were seen as attributes to be valued.

'Keep my picture near your heart, soldier boy.
God will bring you back to me,
Au revoir but not goodbye, soldier boy.'

Lew Brown

10 'Pip, Squeak & Wilfred'
(WW1 Campaign Medals)

Private Horace George Ham

Army Life: Battle of the Somme: Local Lives

Today, there are no longer any survivors of 'The Great War' still alive, but fortunately during the 1990s the Imperial War Museum captured some of their accounts of life during the conflict in a series of Oral Histories. More fortunately for any Bournemouth folk interested in the subject of the war, one of those whose voice echoes down the years, Private Horace George Ham, was Bournemouth born. In a series of three recordings, Horace recounts his early life, his service with the Middlesex Regiment where he was witness to the opening day of the Battle of the Somme, and how for him the war ended while he was in Ireland.

Horace George Ham was born in 'Gloucester', 5 Alum Chine Road, Westbourne on 20 July 1895 where his father Ambrose and mother Mary ran the large Victorian family home as a boarding house. At this time, Horace and his brother Albert attended St. Peter's School in Bournemouth. After school had finished for the day, Horace would be expected to help his parents in the boarding house, and although Horace had ideas of training to be an electrician when he left school at fifteen, he said that his father was 'fixed with the idea' of him going into service in one of the big houses to be found locally. Horace's first position was as a Hall Boy, serving the servants' meals and cleaning at Trafalgar Park in

Wiltshire, and from there he then obtained a post as a Footman with a Mr Penn who had houses in Bournemouth and London. After two years with Mr Penn, Horace went to work at the London Piccadilly home of William Lehman Ashmead Bartlett Burdett-Coutts, an American born Conservative politician who served as an MP from 1885 - 1921.

After war was declared in August 1914, young men in service at all the big country houses were paid a visit and asked to volunteer for the army. As Horace recalled in a 1988 interview with Paul Nixon, 'They came around with a paper while we were working. Would we join? If so, sign the paper.' All the young men of the house were keen to sign, and in January 1915 were asked to report to Whitehall, where they swore an oath of allegiance and took, 'The King's Shilling'. Horace was offered the choice of three regiments: The Essex, The Guards or the Middlesex Regiment. The Battalion offered with the Middlesex Regiment was the 16th (Public Schools) Battalion, and to Horace's thinking, as he had been to a public school in Bournemouth, been a choirboy for seven years and had come from a good home, the Public Schools Battalion made up of 'good, nice fellas' would be the one he would join. The young recruits from that day in January 1915 were told to report back in three days, so Horace came home to Bournemouth to say his goodbyes before leaving for life as an army private. On reporting back for duty, Private Horace Ham was sent to Warlingham in Surrey where the Battalion was formed and basic training, such as learning how to march took place before the battalion was then sent to Clipstone, Nottingham where the Brigade was formed. Approximately six weeks later, in August 1915, the Brigade joined the rest of the Division on Salisbury Plain where they undertook battle training, consisting amongst other things of practice attacks from mock trenches. Horace says how they were one of the lucky battalions, as unlike some battalions they met, they had proper uniforms and were issued with old fashioned Lee Enfield rifles. This 'luck' he puts down to their public school battalion being perceived by those higher up as well educated, bright young men who would be suitable candidates for a commission.

In November 1915, the 16th Middlesex Regiment, as part of the 33rd Division, received their orders to depart for France. On 17th November, Horace landed in Boulogne, and after two nights spent at St Martin's camp was then sent up the line to hold the trenches at Givenchy, Festubert and La Bassee Canal until Christmas 1915. Horace Ham's recall of events and places over seventy years later may have been sketchy, but he clearly remembered the winter of 1915 in the trenches.

(Author's Collection)

Drawing from small sketch book

The winter was cold and wet, the trenches continually full of water and mud; life under constant bombardment was not what he and the four other lads he had teamed up with had expected. Before their first taste of trench life, they had looked forward excitedly to going to France and seeing action against the Germans, but 'it was a different story after we'd been in them!'. He also fondly remembered longer periods of rest in a former girl's school at Bethune, where they could enjoy lovely hot showers.

At some point between March and May 1916, Horace's battalion endured a forced march to the area of the Somme, taking over the trenches at Beaumont Hamel where they remained for a week at a time. Horace's recollection was that this was a comparatively 'quiet' period, although they still suffered constant shelling and attacks by snipers. One such sniper attack resulted in a corporal stood next to Horace being shot in the head. Years later, Horace still mused over that shot, and how being the taller of the men by over six inches, he should have been the easier target. The death of their Corporal made all the lads 'feel very groggy for a bit'.

It is easy to picture this old soldier, a resident in the Star & Garter Home for ex-servicemen, pondering over the events of so long ago. Thinking back, he failed to see the value of duties such as night patrols, which none of the men liked. Made to crawl as near to the front line as they could, the object was to listen to hear what the German's were doing, an objective they all saw as utterly pointless and dangerous. As Horace put it, 'If we'd heard talking, we wouldn't have understood it anyway!' In late June 1916, Horace and the 16th Middlesex were on the move again, this time into trenches ready for the attack scheduled for 1 July - the opening day of the Battle of the Somme. The morning of 1 July saw Horace and his battalion in trenches opposite Hawthorn Ridge where they waited for the signal to attack. The attack was to commence at 07.30 hrs but at 07.20 hrs the first of nineteen mines was detonated underneath the German lines. 40,000 pounds of explosives had been laid beneath the Hawthorn Ridge Redoubt, the early firing of which was seen by many historians later as having contributed to the failure of the British Attack. In Horace's words:

'We saw it go up at 7.20 a.m. and we were supposed to go over at 7.30 a.m. Of course, it was a big mistake. We should have gone over just after the mine went up. They lost a lot of men and there was a hell of a lot blown up, but you see, it was a proper mess up.'

The detonation of the explosives, earlier than scheduled, gave the German's warning of an attack and time to prepare. When the British shelling started, the German troops went down into their dug-outs, and when the shelling stopped, they came up again ready to mow down the advancing troops. In all Horace Ham's recollections, he returns time and again to the feeling that he was 'lucky' during the war, as he put it, 'Every soldier in France looked for a Blighty wound'. As the whistle went at 07.30 hrs on that July morning, and he and his pals made ready to go over the top, Horace was hit by shrapnel in the hip and thus avoided being one of the many who in his words 'fell like ninepins'. Two of his four pals were among the 700 men from the 16th Battalion Middlesex Regiment who were killed that morning. Of the 800 men that left the trenches, only 100 came back. Horace was able to walk about a mile back to the casualty clearing station, from where he was put on a train to a hospital in Boulogne. Back across the channel, Horace was placed on a Red Cross train bound for convalescence in Scotland.

Following a spell of leave back in Bournemouth, he attended the screening of the film 'The Battle of the Somme' at the Electric Theatre. He also spent evenings in the Westbourne Conservative Club, where his father was steward. Horace then received his papers to return to France, but this time with the 12th Middlesex Regiment.

Horace served a further year on the Western Front, in the machine gun section of the regiment. As No. 2 on a Lewis gun, it was his job to load the ammunition. The Battle of Boom Ravine took place in February 1917, during which time Horace was in the second line of advance, and although the British took the ravine, a great many men lost their lives due to the shelling. Horace's memories included watching the large chateau at Achiet-le-Grande, north of Bapaume set afire, one of several that were razed to the ground as part of the retreating German's scorched earth policy.

Private Ham's service on the Western Front finally came to an end on 1 May 1917, when he was wounded again at the second Battle of Arras, when, walking behind a 'creeping barrage' he was hit in the arm. Once again, Horace was put on a hospital train along with hundreds of other wounded men, and after arrival at Southampton port was transferred to a war hospital in Sheffield for a period of three months' recovery. After a period of home leave, letters arrived telling Horace to report to Tipperary, Ireland where as a semi-convalescent he was eventually graded B1 and his fighting days were over. When asked about the political situation in Ireland at that time, Horace replied that the men were all warned about the Sinn Fein; that they should not visit the town alone and that they were given additional ammunition when on guard duty. After five months in Ireland, Horace was asked to join a group of B1 men in the Army Service Corps Remount, stationed at Swaythling, Southampton, grooming and preparing horses ready for going overseas. Despite having no experience with horses, Horace accepted the posting and during his time there, he learnt to ride and also met the girl who was to become his wife.

On the night the Armistice was declared on 11 November 1918, Private Ham was rostered for duty, however, he was keen to meet his girlfriend Mary, and join the celebrations. Horace paid another soldier to take his place and was amongst the thousands on the streets of Southampton 'chock-a-block, shouting, singing, waving flags'. Discharged from the army in 1919, Horace George Ham married Mary Jacobs the same year and returned to life in service, making his way up from Second Head Waiter at the Norfolk Royale Hotel, Bournemouth to Head Waiter at The Raven Hotel, Shrewsbury. Horace and Mary had been married for 61 years when Mary died in 1980. At the Star & Garter Home, Richmond, in January 1995, just six months short of reaching his century, Horace George Ham was reunited with his 'girl'.

Horace George Ham

In July 2016 as part of the commemorations for the Centenary of the First World War, and the Battle of the Somme, a rose bush was planted outside the home in Alum Chine Road where Horace was born. His medals, cap badge and miniature medals, as pictured, are in the possession of the author.

Nearly 20,000 British soldiers were killed on the opening day of the Battle of the Somme, the bloodiest day in the history of the British Army. Amongst that number are at least twelve from Bournemouth.

'Before the world grew mad, the Somme was a placid stream in Picardy'

A D Gristwood

(Author's note: These recollections, are as recalled by Horace then in his 90s, and as such may contain inconsistencies. The oral histories are free to listen to, on the IWM site).

11 Princess Mary's Christmas Tin

Christmas: Tourism: Fundraising: Army Life: Smoking: Troop Morale

Even though England was now at war with Germany, Christmas 1914 in Bournemouth showed very little difference to that of the previous years of peace. In September shortly after the declaration of war, it was reported in the local press that offices and shops were carrying on their business determined to make the best of the situation until the 'champions of England's honour return and resume their duties'. By Christmas the only evidence that something in the town had changed was the shortage of staff in the big stores as men rushed to join up. The shops filled their window displays with the wide range of the goods they had to offer, which that year included British and Allied toys, war games proving the most popular, and all manner of items sure to ease the lot of British troops serving overseas. The wounded soldiers in the local military hospitals were given a Christmas meal and received a small gift, often made by local women. Entertainment was provided in a number of church halls and schools for all the billeted troops in the town; the men of the Royal Engineers being just some of those experiencing the town's hospitality when they sat down to supper and a concert at Stourfield School. With visitors still flocking into the town and the pantomimes attracting full houses, it was business as usual, as confidence in a quick British victory was still high.

For the soldiers serving overseas, the reality of the war was starting to hit home, and their first Christmas away was filled with thoughts of friends and loved ones. Those back home were

encouraged to send cards and gifts to the men who were overjoyed to receive parcels containing tobacco, sweets, plum pudding and even games. In December 1914 the wife of Sir John French, British Commander-in-Chief asked the nation's women to knit and post 250,000 mufflers to the front, not only to keep the men warm, but to ensure that no one went without a Christmas gift. Regimental Christmas cards began to appear displaying pride in the unit, decorated with the battles and campaigns taken part in, along with others that displayed the black humour often associated with the 'Tommy' on the front. For the men, the sending of Christmas cards created a sense of normality and familiarity – a link to home and those that waited for them. Christmas dinner for those lucky to be away from the front line was a basic but traditional dinner. However, for those in the trenches it was the usual bland rations.

The Christmas gift to all those serving with the armed forces of the British Empire was the brainchild of Mary, Princess Royal, the 17 year old daughter of King George V. Her intention was that 'every sailor afloat and every soldier at the front' should receive a gift on Christmas Day 1914. This was later extended to include everyone wearing the King's uniform on that day. In total, over two and a half million. In October 1914, Princess Mary launched her appeal to fund the Christmas gift with adverts placed in newspapers asking for donations to the Soldiers and Sailors Christmas fund. A letter released by Buckingham Palace and signed by the Princess read:

'I want you now to help me to send a Christmas present from the whole nation to every sailor afloat and every soldier at the front. I am sure that we should all be happier to feel that we helped to send our little token of love and sympathy on Christmas morning, something that would be useful and of permanent value, and the making of which may be the means of providing employment in trades adversely affected by the war. Could there be anything more likely to hearten them in their struggle than a present received straight from home on Christmas Day. Please will you help me?'

In total £152,691 was raised, and the committee overseeing the project agreed that the production of the tins – silver for Officers and brass for all other ranks – would bear the image of Princess Mary and be decorated with military and imperial symbols. The contents decided upon at the outset were to be: an ounce of tobacco, or a packet of cigarettes in yellow monogrammed wrappers, a cigarette lighter, a Christmas card and a photo of the Princess. For non-smokers the tobacco product would be replaced with chocolate and/or lemon drops. The small, simple card would bear the monogram of Princess Mary, as would each individual cigarette.

However, the idea for a standard list of contents for the boxes ran into difficulties when the committee was faced with objection and strong representation from other groups, and with problems with the supply of the items. It was felt that both the smokers' and non-smokers' gifts were unsuitable for nurses at the front, therefore they were given the standard gift box and chocolate. Representation was made to the committee that alternative gifts should be made available for non-smokers, so it was agreed that instead they could receive acid tablets, and a monogrammed writing case containing pencils, paper and envelopes. The committee was then asked to consider not only the dietary requirements of the differing religious faiths of the serving men, but also the other ethnic groups that made up part of the British forces. Finally, it was decided that the Gurkhas would have the same standard box; those of the Sikh religion, a box filled with sweets and a box of spices; all other Indian troops, a box containing cigarettes, sweets, spices. The high numbers of standard items required, inevitably led to problems of supply, and it is not unusual today to find nonstandard items such as pencils, combs and knives. Sailor's boxes that should have received a lighter, often contained a substitute bullet pencil in a monogrammed silver cartridge case.

It soon became apparent that the large number due to receive the Princess Mary's Christmas Gift would make it impossible to manufacture, fill and distribute to the recipients in time for Christmas Day 1914. Therefore, they were divided into three levels of priority:

Class A – All troops at the Front in France; the Navy including those on minesweepers and in dockyards; the wounded in hospital and men on leave; prisoners and men interned whose gift was reserved; nurses at the Front and members of the French Mission. Widows or parents of men killed in the first months of the war were also included. Those in Class A would receive their gift on or as near to Christmas Day 1914 as possible.

Class B – All British, Colonial and Indian troops serving overseas, not eligible to be in Class A.

Class C – All troops stationed in the British Isles.

Although 400,000 were delivered by Christmas Day, the gifts for Classes B & C were not sent out until January 1915, thereby contained a Happy New Year Card. Sourcing the brass for the tins became a problem after May 1915 when the RMS Lusitania was sunk by a German U-boat, carrying 45 tons of brass strip destined for making the boxes. For this reason, in addition to the stretched postal service, distribution of all the gifts was not completed until 1920.

Gradually over the next few years, as Germany's blockade tightened its grip, the people of Bournemouth witnessed changes both in the retail sector and in domestic life, which made their traditional Christmas a thing of the past. Although the period of 1915 -1916 had seen new department stores such as Bobbys and Woolworths opening in the square, newly implemented lighting restrictions meant that people stayed away from the town after dark, and on weekdays the shops began to close early. Christmas shoppers were therefore advised to make the most of the daylight hours and to shop early for their gifts. However, trade was still at this time brisk, and large hotels reported few vacancies, despite the restrictions on travel caused in 1916 by soldiers on leave having priority on trains. All the theatre performances played to full houses, but the main members of the cast still found time to entertain the wounded either in the hospitals or at special performances. At Christmas 1916, 1000 of the wounded from all the local hospitals were given free seats to see the pantomime Sleeping Beauty, organised by the Theatre Royal.

(Courtesy of Alwyn Ladell)

Crag Head Hospital Christmas Card 1917

By Christmas 1917, the German attempts to starve the British into submission which at one point saw just six weeks of food remaining, necessitated the introduction of compulsory food rationing. Long queues were seen across the country for basic food items like margarine, sugar and milk. The *Bournemouth Echo* ran adverts by The Master Butchers advising that they could not guarantee that they would be able to meet demand. Milk deliveries would be cut to one delivery a day. The atmosphere in the town was subdued, and although visitors came, the thought of entering another year with no end to the war in sight and the growing casualty lists, left many in no mood to celebrate.

A year later, following The Armistice agreement, Bournemouth was once again celebrating Christmas in full swing. The war was finally over, and the men were coming home! Street lamps and shop windows were lit again. The hotels enjoyed a period akin to that of the pre-war period, in addition to which, all the theatres and attractions were full. As in every year of the war, the hospitals put on entertainment and provided small gifts to their wounded and residents opened their homes to any soldier still stationed in the town.

1918 had been both a time of much grieving in the town for the local lives lost, and a time for beginning to look forward with hope. The 'Christmas tin' of 1914 became a treasured item in the homes of those who had received them and many an old soldier would go on to store their medals in them and other small reminders of fighting in the trenches and comrades lost.

'May God protect you and bring you safely home'

King George V (1914)

12 Red Cross Nursing Cup

Military Hospitals: Nursing: War Casualties: Local Lives

After the declaration of war on Germany, Bournemouth was one of several seaside towns approached by the War Office and asked to provide accommodation for both sick and wounded soldiers. The Royal Victoria and West Hants Hospital, later to become Boscombe Military Hospital, was one of the first ready by September 1914 to receive the wounded. Following a grant from the Mayor's Local War Fund of £750, marquees were erected in the grounds to make three additional wards built on raised boarded floors, one containing thirty beds, and the others eighteen apiece. The first wounded to be cared for at the Boscombe Hospital, were a group of one hundred British soldiers from the Battle of Arras who arrived by ambulance train at Boscombe Railway station on 9 October 1914. Met by members of the local St John Ambulance, a number were walking wounded, but some needed to be stretchered across Ashley Road to the hospital.

Crag Head Red Cross Hospital in Manor Road, Bournemouth was another hospital that had been prepared from September to receive patients. Crag Head had been built in the later 1800s and saw numerous visits by foreign Royalty, before being lent to the British Red Cross for use as a hospital in August 1914. In an article entitled 'Romance of Modern Nursing' published in the *Bournemouth Graphic* on 25 September 1914, it describes the 'transformation   of the largest residence in Bournemouth into a Red Cross Hospital'. Every item required to fit out the hospital,

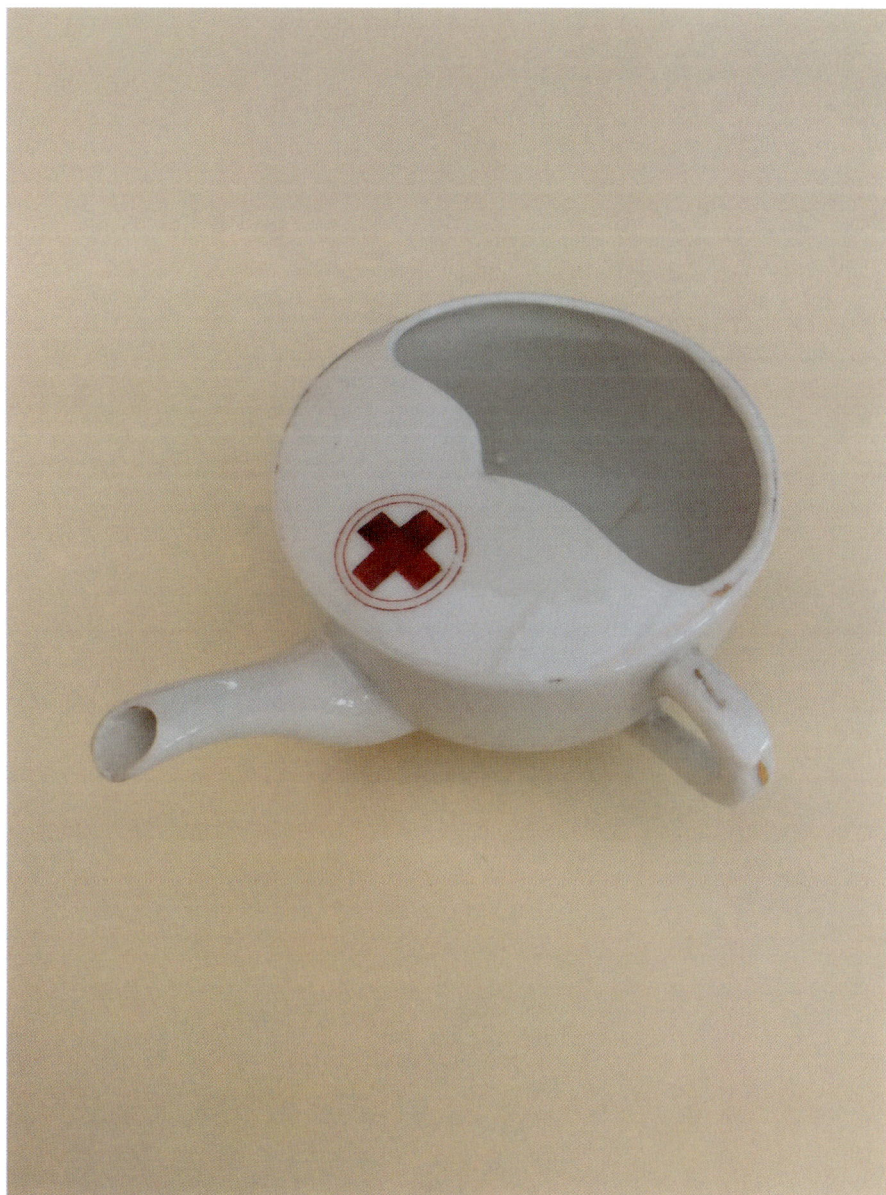

from kitchen equipment to beds was provided by the generosity of the Bournemouth public. Although its first one hundred patients arrived at Central Station on 14 October 1914, it was in December 1914 that it was taken over by the War Office as a hospital for acute medical cases, largely due to the large number of troops billeted in the town who needed medical care. From October 1914 through to July 1915, 837 patients were treated at Crag Head, which had its own operating theatre covering the fourteen wards. By June 1917, the number who received care at the hospital had risen in line with the number of battle casualties to just over 2,000.

By the end of 1914, Bournemouth was receiving a steady stream of wounded men, therefore additional beds were required for soldiers from all the Commonwealth forces. The Mont Dore Hotel (now Bournemouth's Town Hall), was converted into a hospital for Indian troops after being requisitioned by the War Office in November 1914. One hundred men, mostly suffering from shrapnel injuries and bayonet wounds arrived at the Mont Dore, along with members of the Madras Infantry Regiment to look after them. Further contingents of wounded Gurkha & Sikh troops arrived in the town in January 1915, many suffering from frostbite. The Battle of Neuve Chappelle in March brought over one hundred Indian troops to the Mont Dore Military Hospital for treatment and recuperation.

All the hospitals were staffed by trained nurses, some of whom were members of the Red Cross or St John Ambulance. When a new auxiliary hospital opened, the Red Cross were asked to provide the nursing staff, who would normally be locally resident. In 1909, the Voluntary Aid Detachment were formed to supplement the Territorial Army Medical Services. VADs as they came to be known, had to pass exams set by either the St John Ambulance or the British Red Cross Society. Those trained by the Red Cross wore a red cross on either their armband or apron, and likewise those trained by the St John Ambulance wore an eight-pointed star on theirs. As stated in *Bournemouth and the First World War* by M A Edgington, life for the nursing staff in hospitals such as Crag Head was not easy. A probationer's trial period lasted three months, the first month of which was as a ward maid whose duties included cleaning the wards, preparing meals and other tasks akin to those in domestic service. The second month would be spent on the wards undertaking basic nursing duties, and night duty was the 'promotion' in the third month from 20.00 hrs until 08.00 hrs the following morning. Usual shifts in the hospitals were either 08.30 hrs to 14.00 hrs, or 14.00 hrs to 20.30 hrs. During the war years, competitions were held regularly to test the knowledge of the VADs and ensure competence, but also had a secondary purpose in that they encouraged funding from local residents. Questions asked might include:

How would you prepare a patient and a room for a major operation?
How would you prepare a linseed meal poultice or a mustard poultice?
What are bedsores and how would you prevent and treat them?

Prior to February 1915, the Belgian wounded were treated at Grata Quies, a private home originally lent as accommodation for Belgian Refugees, but later equipped as a hospital. The first Belgian soldiers arrived at Grata Quies in the winter of 1914, and until it was decided by the Belgian authorities in 1915 to no longer send their wounded to the town, over 394 men from the Belgian Army received treatment in Bournemouth's hospitals and nursing homes. Grata Quies, in Western Avenue, was transferred to the War Office for the nursing of British soldiers in November 1915.

The Battle of the Somme in July 1916 inevitably led to a large number of battle casualties arriving for nursing care in Bournemouth. The sheer number arriving by Red Cross ambulance train to either Boscombe, Central, or West stations required those controlling the flow to adopt an efficient set of procedures for dealing with the casualties. Ambulances arrived at their designated station after word had been received that a train was expected. Once there, the Red Cross members would be assigned their duties, either unloading the wounded from the train, staying at the station to load the ambulances, or travelling with the wounded to unload them at the hospitals. The men travelling in the front carriages of the train would in general be the walking wounded. The 'cot cases' suffering from more serious wounds were lifted off the train, their injuries assessed, and then taken to whichever hospital was decided by members of the staff in charge of the military hospitals. Patients destined for Boscombe Military Hospital had to be carried through crowds of well-wishers, before crossing the road to the reception hall. Often those sent to be nursed at the Mont Dore would have to be carried up the curved staircase, due to the lift being out of order. In the three weeks following the Battle of the Somme, some 400 men were admitted to local hospitals, arriving daily on ambulance trains that would continue arriving throughout the day, often until 2 a.m. During the years 1914 -1916, over fifty Red Cross trains carrying British wounded arrived at Boscombe station, and by the end of 1918 this number had risen to 156.

The number of Bournemouth nurses who either worked in the local hospitals or overseas in the casualty clearing stations is unknown. Only three with a Bournemouth connection are known to have died during the war years, and while they may have died in service, none were directly killed as a result of enemy action:

Sister Emily Helena Cole – daughter of Mrs E H Cole, 46 Charminster Road, died on the 21 February 1915 aged 32 while nursing in France with the Queen Alexandra's Imperial Military Nursing Service. Emily embarked for France soon after the outbreak of war and worked as a staff nurse at the 14th General Hospital, Boulogne. Sister Cole is buried in Wimereux Communal Cemetery, the same cemetery as Lt. Col. John McCrae, author of *In Flanders Fields*. Unusually for a Commonwealth War Graves Cemetery, the headstones all lie flat due to the sandy nature of the soil. She is also one of the 1,300 named on the The Nursing Memorial in the National Memorial Arboretum.

VAD Emily Mary Elwes - who died in service in Bournemouth on 19 March 1917 is remembered on the WW1 memorial in St Swithin's Church, Gervis Road, and on the The Nursing Memorial in the National Memorial Arboretum dedicated on 4 June 2018.

VAD Norah Kidson – who died in service in Bournemouth in December 1917.

(Courtesy of Alwyn Ladell)

Patients and Nurses Crag Head Hospital

In his local studies guide (published in 1985) on Bournemouth during the First World War, Mike Edgington (having access to the record of work done in the town by the St John Ambulance 1914-1919) provided a detailed account of their work alongside accounts of all the war hospitals in the local area. While this author has remained conscious of not replicating his work, there are some interesting statistics from the publication worth mentioning:

Boscombe Military Hospital

Between October 1914 and December 1915, over 3,000 military personnel had been treated with only twelve deaths. A later report in 1916 stated that 801 patients had been returned to their units as fit for active service and that there had only been seven deaths. Meanwhile, a total of 1,246 military in-patients had been treated. On 20 January 1916, a fund-raising event took place to provide the 'Nurse Cavell' bed in the hospital, in response to and in memory of the British Nurse executed by the Germans on 12 October 1915. Administration, i.e. admissions, pay, and travel for all the local military hospitals came under Boscombe Military Hospital. In July 1918 the main hospital reverted to treating civilians.

Mont Dore Military Hospital

From November 1914 until November 1915, the hospital was specifically used to treat Indian troops who would then go on to convalesce at Barton-on-Sea. From 1915, British, Australian, and New Zealand wounded replaced the Indian Troops, the running of the hospital falling to members of the Royal Army Medical Corps after July 1916. In 1918, the Mont Dore became a convalescent home for officers, and the existing patients transferred to other hospitals across the country. Many of the officers had been repatriated from prisoner of war camps. The Mont Dore closed in 1919, and after purchase from the Corporation, reopened as the Town Hall in 1921.

Crag Head Red Cross Hospital

In 1915, there were fourteen qualified nursing staff under the control of the Matron, covering the four floors and twenty VAD probationers. Due to its spacious gardens, the recuperating soldiers could sit out in fine weather or make use of the large conservatory at other times. These gardens were also used for fund raising fetes, not just in aid of the hospitals but for other war causes as well. Crag

Head closed as a hospital at the end of 1918, following which the equipment was sold at auction in February 1919.

These are just three of the hospitals used in the Bournemouth area to treat casualties from the majority of Commonwealth countries who got caught up in one of the greatest conflicts of our time. For information on all the military and auxiliary hospitals used in the town from 1914 -1918, see *Bournemouth and the First World War* by M A Edgington.

'As the stars in a dark sky they lit up our world'

The Nursing Memorial

13 Coin Bracelet

Co. Quartermaster Sergeant Harry Reginald Gifford

Trench Art: Army Life: WW1 Souvenirs: Local Lives

'Harry's Bracelet' comes under the umbrella term of WW1 'Trench Art', a name given to a variety of items, mostly decorative, which were produced during or just after the First World War. Although commonly considered to have been made by serving soldiers or prisoners of war, in reality only a small number of items would have been made in the front line. The art of making items, now called trench art, started before WW1, but it is certainly during the period of 1914 – 1919 that the fashion for creating souvenir objects from re-purposed bullets, spent charges and shells, coins and even animal bone came into its own. Items commonly found by collectors include ashtrays, letter knives, shell vases and models of tanks and airplanes. However, embroidered items such as pin cushions and love tokens also come under the generic term of trench art. Although it is possible that a few smaller pieces, especially those made with animal bone, may have been made by men in the quieter periods in the trenches, it is more likely that trench art items were made in the workshops behind the front line. It is here that the materials, skill, machinery and time would be found and the workers more than happy to meet the demand from the troops for souvenirs in exchange for money or cigarettes.

The villages in and around the Western Front suffered badly from the conflict. Many French and Belgian civilians were displaced by the war, and the loss of not only their homes but their

means of earning a living caused significant hardship to those families already surviving on the edge of poverty. A cottage industry therefore sprung up crafting decorative pieces and embroidered postcards, the latter proving to be a popular novelty amongst soldiers thinking of their loved ones back home.

In the post war years in England, many large department stores offered to turn soldiers' war souvenirs into functional items for the home. If the returning soldier had no such item, the store could provide it, which may account for larger trench art items such as dinner gongs and vases made from cannon shells, which would have proved difficult to transport home.

The rise in popularity of battlefield visits during the 1920s and 1930s created a new manufacturing industry for the French and Belgians, when by making full use of the spent detritus of the war they were able to offer a full range of souvenirs to the visiting ex-soldier or grieving relative. These pieces would usually be inscribed with the place or battle memorable to each purchaser. The practice of reworking original WW1 shell casings still found in the fields of the conflict continues to this day. The rise in battlefield tourism, due in part to the centenary commemorations, has generated fresh demand.

There are considered to be four categories of WW1 Trench Art of interest to the collector or student of First World War social history:

1   Items made by soldiers – Small items, often cruder in design or inscription, such as rings or knives made by the soldiers in the front line or support trenches. Items made by wounded soldiers as therapy i.e. embroidered pieces, also come under this category.

2   Items made by prisoners of war or internees – decorative items made during periods of free time, and exchanged for food, money or privileges.

3   Civilian made souvenirs – generally considered to be decorative items made during the war by the civilian population in and around the areas of the conflict, but

can also include items made by sweethearts at home as a 'keep safe' keepsake for their fighting man. This category also covers those items made post war when the villagers reclaimed their communities. In order to satisfy the growing demand by pilgrims and tourists, enterprising individuals from these communities recycled discarded war debris into souvenirs bearing the crest of the town/village where produced.

4   Commercially produced souvenirs – After the war, tonnes of surplus material was sold by the Government and converted into battlefield souvenirs. This was particularly prevalent when ships involved in action were broken down and the wood turned into miniature barrels or letterboxes. Wooden items from ships involved in major events, such as the Battle of Jutland, featuring the name of the ship on a small plaque became extremely popular and still are for the collector of naval memorabilia.

Company Quartermaster Sergeant Harry Reginald Gifford was born in Pokesdown, Bournemouth in 1891. He was the only son of Henry and Charlotte who in 1901, along with Harry and his sisters Lily and May, were living in Christchurch Road, Bournemouth. The service record for Harry Gifford no longer exists, but by the 1911 census Harry had joined the Somerset Light Infantry as a Private and he and the other men from the 1st Battalion are recorded as living at the Verne Citadel on Portland. One of the other men listed with Harry is William Facey, also from Bournemouth, and John Blake from Upper Parkstone.

What is known from Harry's medal index card is that after enlisting at Winchester he then 'entered the theatre of war' in France on 21 August 1914, less than three weeks after the outbreak of WW1. By the time of his death, Harry had attained the rank of Company Quartermaster Sergeant, a non-commissioned officer in charge of supplies.

While we do not know by record the course of Harry's service during the First World War, his trench art bracelet is more than just a decorative souvenir, it is its own unique service record bearing as it does the name of actions seen inscribed on the back of the French, Belgian and German coins that make up the bracelet. Without having first hand family knowledge, it cannot be established whether it was Harry himself who had the bracelet made, or his wife Alice Beatrice (who the Civil Marriage Registration shows he married in January 1918) after his death.

Eight silver coins make up Harry's bracelet; five French 50 centimes, one dated 1895 and one 1917; two larger coins, a French Franc and a Belgian coin and one German aluminium 1917 Pfennig. The coin on the clasp on the right-hand side, is also a German Pfennig. On the reverse in chronological order are inscribed the following places/battles on the Western Front:

Mons 1914, Marne 1914, Ypres 1914, Ypres 1915, Soome *(sic)* 1916, Longamark *(sic)* 1917, Cambrai 1917

The misspelling of the words Somme and Langemarck add a certain poignancy to the bracelet, which is further heightened by the inscriptions on either end. The final French centime before the pin of the clasp is inscribed 'Married January 1918' and on the reverse of the clasp itself - 'Died November 1918'.

Harry Reginald Gifford died in Bournemouth on 14 November 1918, and is buried in the Commonwealth War Graves section of East Cemetery, Gloucester Road. Whether Harry died from wounds received overseas or during the Spanish influenza epidemic raging through the country is unrecorded. As there are no further battles inscribed after Cambrai, which took place in November 1917, it is entirely possible that he was wounded then or shortly after. The monies due to him at the time of his death amount to thirty four pounds and eighteen shillings, which was later paid to his widow Alice. That Harry, after surviving for the entire period of the war, should die three days after the Armistice was declared, and only ten months into his marriage, was a cruel twist of fate.

(Author's Collection)

CQMS Sergeant Harry Gifford Grave

**'And I shall find the white May-blossoms sweet,
Though you have passed away'**

Vera Brittain

14 Crested China Bi-plane

Aviation: RFC: Souvenir Manufacture: Crested China

Aviation was very much still in its infancy at the outbreak of the First Word War. The first powered flight by the Wright Brothers had only taken place just over a decade before and the practical uses of aircraft in a war setting were at first seen to be limited to those of reconnaissance and ariel photography over the battlefield. Air flight was fast becoming the way of the future and as a result the demand for pilot training in both the commercial and military world escalated. Started by Yorkshire born Frederick Etches, an experienced pilot, the Bournemouth Aviation Company (BAC) opened its new aerodrome at Talbot Village in November 1915 purely as a commercial enterprise, giving exhibitions of flying – Admission 6d and 1/- and passenger flights from £3. In order to meet the demand for pilot training the BAC turned their attention to developing a Flying School which went on to train some of the leading lights in the aviation world. As the First World War lengthened and the potential of armed aircraft was realised, the Royal Flying Corps (RFC), formed in 1912, needed training schools for their future pilots. The Flying School at Talbot Village and later Ensbury Park, run by the BAC, soon earned a reputation as 'the best equipped flying school outside London'. One of only a few flying schools across the country, sixteen future pilots for not only the RFC but the Belgian Flying Corps began their training there in 1916, flying Cauldron bi-planes under the tutelage of Chief Instructor Edgar Brynildsen. On 30 December 1916, the BAC purchased Ensbury Park Farm, previously sold at auction for

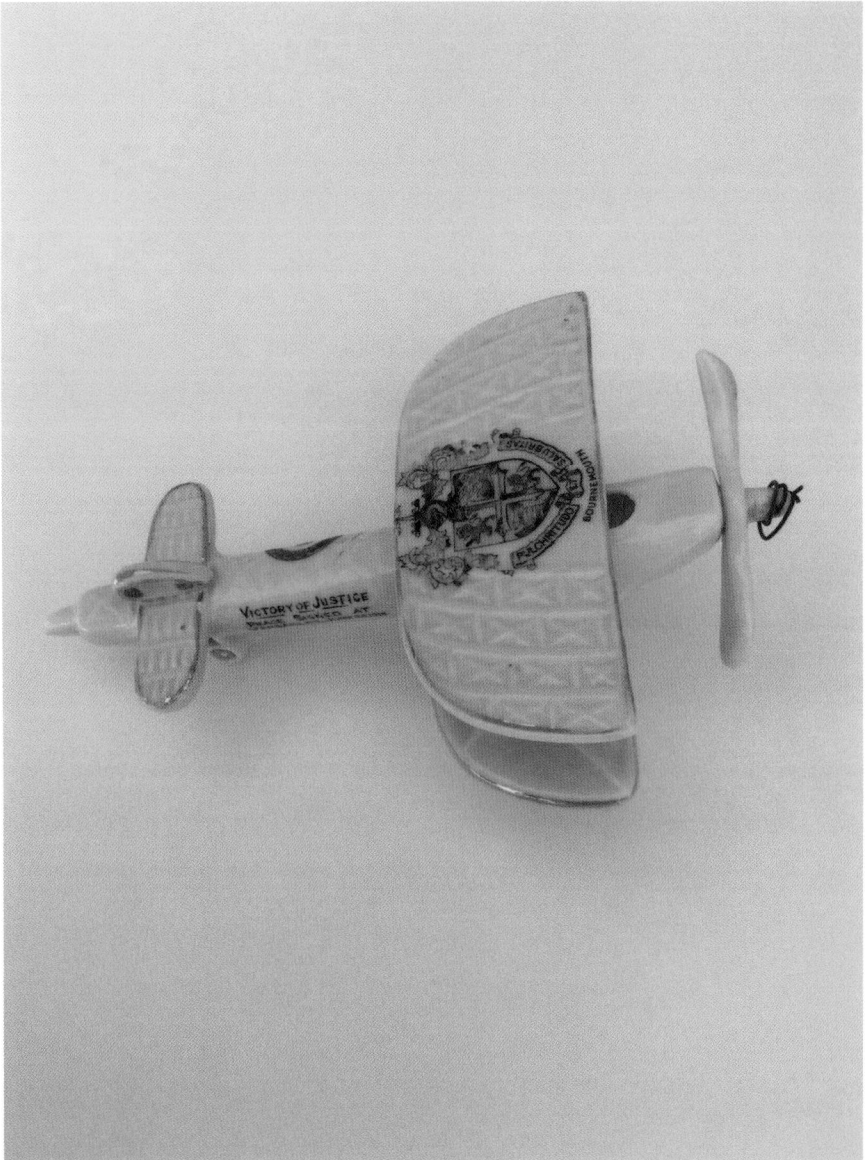

£8,600, after which the training school relocated there, as the flat, level fields with clear approaches, laying as they did on a plateau 100 feet above sea level, provided ideal conditions for an airfield. The airfield and training school were requisitioned by the RFC early in 1917, and pilot training continued at what was now called RFC Winton.

During the training school years 1916 – 1918, inevitably several crashes were witnessed in the Bournemouth area, some of them fatal. The son of a previous Mayor of the town, Second Lieutenant Edward Rebbeck, flew into Bournemouth on 24 April 1916 on a training flight. While taking off again, his plane crashed just outside the aerodrome, then still at Talbot Village. He was buried with full military honours at Wimborne Road Cemetery. In early June 1918, Second Lieutenant Leonard Messenger was found unconscious by a local farmer near the wreckage of his aircraft on Redhill common, and later died in Boscombe Hospital. The inquest into his death, held in Bournemouth and reported in the *Bournemouth Guardian* on 13 July concluded that he died due to injuries 'which were consistent with his having fallen from a plane'. One witness called to give evidence reported that Second Lieutenant Messenger, Royal Field Artillery, but attached to the RAF, 'left his camp, flying alone, on 3 June'. A second witness flying in another aircraft stated that he saw the machine fall. Leonard Messenger is buried in Bournemouth East Cemetery.

'Dashing young pilots' of the RFC and later the Royal Air Force (RAF) often earned a reputation for performing flying stunts and 'showing off'. This was often encouraged as a means of fundraising. At the garden fete held at Crag Head hospital in 1916, an aircraft from Talbot Village aerodrome flew low over the crowd dropping cigarettes and flowers. Inevitably, these acts of bravado often resulted in needless fatalities. A spectacular crash over the Lansdowne area on 22 July 1918 was rumoured to have been caused by one such display of showmanship and exhibitionism in order to impress a young woman. Major John Lowcock, DSO, MC was the pilot at the controls of a Bristol fighter, when, flying too low at approximately 100ft, the wing of the aircraft struck the top of a tree and plunged to the ground. Eye witnesses disagreed with the official report and stated that the plane had made several passes at fifty feet, in order to 'buzz' the house of a girlfriend. Petrol from the crashed airplane leaked into the tram lines in Christchurch road and caught fire. The recommendation made by the jury at the inquest into Major Lowcock's death was that low-level flying should be banned over built up areas.

(Public Domain Image – wikimedia commons)

Royal Flying Corps Poster

Bournemouth's connection to the fast-moving development of the air industry during WW1 was not limited to training pilots. Several local engineering companies were given contracts to make gun mountings and aircraft parts, one becoming an aircraft workshop in Wharfdale Road, and wooden spare/replacement parts were built by woodworking firms in the area. In August 1918 in response to the Ministry of Munition's urgent need for women workers between the ages of 18 and 35 to help build aeroplanes for what had been since April, the Royal Air Force, an exhibition was held in the town showcasing the work done in factories.

Although never attaining a VC for a 'home grown' Bournemouth pilot, the public were quick to claim connection to Lieutenant William Leefe Robinson RFC. Lt. Robinson, born in India, spent six years in the town as a child and later returned to attend Stirling House, Manor Road, a coaching establishment for those who would later enter Sandhurst. Rudyard Kipling's son 'Jack' is also known to have received military coaching in the town, in all probability at the same establishment, before receiving his commission to the Irish Guards despite his poor vision. William Robinson won his VC on the night of 2/3 September 1916 for shooting down enemy airships during the Zeppelin raid over London. When, during the screening of the film, 'The Battle of the Somme' in September 1916, Lieutenant Robinson's picture was projected, the crowd reacted with cheering and applause, just as they would have if he had truly been a Bournemouthian.

Several models of British aircraft were produced as part of the China Manufacturers' WW1 heraldic china range, although the structure of the early planes makes realistic reproduction not easy to attain. However, Robert Southall does say in his book *Take Me Back To Dear Old Blighty,* 'Of the fifteen different models of aircraft recorded, most with some accuracy, can be placed in the war years'. Both bi-plane and monoplane models were produced with either fixed or moveable propellers. Of these, the monoplane was made by far more manufacturers, who in 1915 added RFC roundels and colours to their models to make identification that much easier. Most were based on the Bleriot monoplane, of which few saw action as a war plane. The decision to concentrate on this model may have been due to the popularity of Bleriot after his channel crossing flight in 1909. Models of bi-planes, although produced in far less quantity are more varied in style. Difficulties were faced by most manufacturers in modelling the two separate wings, which led some potters to fill in the space between, thus overcoming the problem. Carlton and Savoy China produced their versions with separate wings, which today makes them the more sought after. Carlton added two versions of their bi-plane, one was based on the Sopwith Strutter (registered in September 1916), the other, (as main picture) from the author's collection, which was sold by Beales of Bournemouth. It obviously dates from the post war period, bearing as it does the inscription:

'Victory of Justice. Peace Signed at Versailles, 28th June 1919'

Arcadian produced a model in December 1916, based on a Sopwith Pup. Grafton's biplane resembles a BE2c, and Shelly China's model from early 1918 was based on a Sopwith Camel. Those models of aircraft found marked 'Foreign' or 'Made in Germany' were produced in Germany during the 1920s.

Ensbury Park Aerodrome was handed back to Bournemouth Aviation Company in May 1919, after which they began a passenger service from Bournemouth to London in addition to the pleasure flights, but by 1922 the Aerodrome that had played its part in the air history of WW1 had been turned over to become a race course.

'Thank God men cannot fly, and lay waste the sky as well as the earth'

Henry David Thoreau

15 Postcards from the Front

Leonard John Shirley

Army Postal Service: Army Life: Postcards: Romance: Local Lives

Receiving post from home, however mundane or trivial, was vital to the morale of the fighting men in all areas of conflict during WW1. The joy of getting a letter was only equalled by 'the glumness of those who received none'. In 1913, with the war clouds gathering, the War Office, in readiness, created the formation of a military postal unit – The Royal Engineers, Special Reserve Postal Section. All the men were recruited solely from Post Office personnel. On the declaration of war on Germany, the unit consisted of 300 men, but by the end of the war in 1918 this figure had risen to over 3,000. To handle the volume of mail, a new central sorting office was opened in Regent's Park in December 1914. At its peak it sorted over twelve million letters/postcards and one million parcels each week. Throughout the duration of the war, a daily train consisting of approximately thirty boxcars pulled into Victoria Station at 11.00 hrs. It would then be loaded with the bags of outgoing mail, and at 11.30 hrs it would leave on time for Folkestone. The first five months of the war saw 2,000 bags of mail sent to the men of the British Expeditionary Force.

Sorting staff at the new central Home Depot quickly became adept at sorting the post by numbers and initials rather than the more customary streets and towns. At the depot, bags of mail would be sorted for each unit serving overseas and given a code label

denoting the Field Post Office to which it would be forwarded. On arrival in France, the bags of mail were checked and weighed at the Base Post Office, then sent on to a railhead where lorries would transport them to supply refilling points situated a few miles behind the lines. Horse drawn wagons would then collect the bags and deliver to the relevant Field Post Office, from where the mail would then be sorted into companies and platoons. Fatigue parties and orderlies from each unit would arrive to collect the post and take it back up the line for distribution to the men eagerly waiting for a word from a loved one or friend - 'If friends at home only realised... they would not omit to write to their soldiers' (Basil Clarke).

When the BEF first arrived in France, the troops were granted a privileged rate of 1d to send a letter home, the normal rate being 2d, but during the first few weeks of the war it became increasingly difficult to obtain stamps and if unstamped post arrived home the recipient would be required to pay the postage. It soon became apparent to the postal authorities in Britain that the volume of unstamped mail arriving from France was proving uneconomical with regard to collecting the postage due from families. In August 1914 the Government decided that in future all letters sent by soldiers on active service could be sent back to Britain without payment by either the sender or the recipient. This directive only applied to troops actually overseas although a concession was later made to men about to be posted, who wanted to write a letter or card of farewell.

There had long been a tradition of conveying a secret message on postal items by the positioning of the stamp. In the days before the advent of text messages enabled the discreet sending of a romantic message, the positioning of stamps was seized upon by the men of the BEF and their loved ones as a small way of overcoming the censorship regulations. A stamp placed upside down in the top left corner meant 'I love you'; one on its side 'when shall I see you?'; upright in line with the surname 'accept my love'. This practice was encouraged by postcard manufacturers of the day to boost sales. However, with the introduction of free post for those on active service, stamps were no longer required. Nonetheless, the average 'Tommy' was determined to continue the practice by buying a French stamp and positioning it according to the 'Language of Stamps'.

Leonard John Shirley was born in Holdenhurst in 1889 to bricklayer James, and Agnes. In 1901, the family, which included his two brothers, Edward Albert and Wallis Rupert and his sister Stella Irene, were living at 242 Wimborne Road, Winton. As a boy, Leonard attended St John's School in Moordown, and by 1911 he was employed as a book packer and porter, still living in Wimborne Road, and playing in a local band during his spare time. By the time he enlisted in the Hussars on 26 August 1914, his family had moved further down Wimborne Road to number 426 (now a white cottage near to the corner of Elmes Road). When 'Len' starts his correspondence with 'Skiddles' – Kate Dunford, he is Trooper 15562 of the 15th Hussars, based at Longmoor in Hampshire. Kate, born in 1891 in Moordown, is living not far from Leonard at number 317 Wimborne Road. During this time she is employed as a servant. The first postcards to Len sent in November 1914 are written as one friend to another using the language one would expect, and signed off from Kit or Kitty. If the position of the stamp on one is deliberate however, the language of stamps would give its meaning as 'Accept My Love'. While at Longmoor, Leonard receives a postcard from his mother in Bournemouth, advising him that she will be visiting him on Tuesday, 'can't get there soon enough, love Mother'

Leonard Shirley's service record indicates that he was transferred to the 3rd Battalion of the York & Lancaster Regiment in June 1915, and it is with them that he landed in France on 21 June 1915. Len's first postcard to Kate from France is dated 27 July 1915, and is still very much a formal card, although censorship would not allow for anything different on a postcard. From 6 June 1915 Leonard was back in England convalescing after being wounded by a bayonet in the thigh, and although the next postcard to him is not dated, given that it sends New Year's greetings, it can be assumed that this was January 1916. Things between Len and

Kate have now moved on. The card is now covered in kisses and is the first one that is signed off with the pet name 'Skiddles', a term Len continues to use when he is sent back to France on the 23 February 1916, from where he posts her subsequent cards dated 6 March 1916. As Leonard was on active service in France, the only postcards he can find to send are French. Whether he or his 'Skiddles' understood the meaning of the words on them, we will never know. The translation of one - 'My soul is embalmed, and from the bottom of my heart awaits the divine hour, the hour of happiness', the second – 'I cannot forget you anymore. Let me hope for hope' give voice to a young man asking his sweetheart to wait for him.

Sadly, 'Skiddles' did not get to see her 'dear Len' again, as on 21 April 1916, Private Leonard John Shirley was killed in action aged 27. His effects, including his £17 wages, were returned home on 7 July 1916. Leonard Shirley is buried in Essex Farm Cemetery, near the village of Boezinge in Belgium. Essex Farm was the location of a casualty clearing station during the war, not far from the Yser Canal which formed part of the front line between April 1915 and August 1917.

Kate Dunford later married Bertram Newman in 1924, and they subsequently had a son called Eric. In 1971 in Bristol 'Skiddles' died aged 78.

'Not Forgotten Until The Day Break And The Shadows Flee Away'

Inscription on the Headstone of Pte. L J Shirley

(Author's Collection)

Private Leonard John Shirley Grave – Essex Farm Cemetery

16 Ration Cards

Rationing: Life in the Town: Local Lives

During the first few years of WW1, food was still in adequate supply for the people of Bournemouth, and any consideration given to it was aimed at finding additional supplies to feed the wounded in the local hospitals or those serving their country. Schemes such as the National Egg Collection of 1915 tasked itself with collecting and delivering newly laid eggs free of charge to wounded servicemen, whilst the Vegetable Products Committee set up a depot in The Triangle to receive donations of money or vegetables to be sent to the men on merchant boats in the North Sea. During 1916, business in the town was still brisk, with the majority of the hotels and boarding houses not noticing any detrimental effects due to the war. The only change really evident was at Easter, when there was an absence of hot cross buns, and German-made Easter Eggs.

However, all this was to change in 1917, when the Germans began their policy of unrestricted submarine warfare by their U-boat fleet which aimed at starving the British into submission. The sinking of a great many of the merchant ships carrying supplies to England created the need for the Government to develop a strategy in order to ensure that the British population did not go short of food. In December 1916, the Ministry of Food began to encourage cultivation of every piece of available land. Any land earmarked for building was divided into allotments, and along with neglected gardens, was cleared, dug over and planted with vegetables. In Bournemouth, The Women's Emergency Corps arranged for the gardens of serving soldiers to be cultivated for the specific benefit

of the family. Four hundred plots were being cultivated by April 1917 with this figure more than doubling by April 1918.

Early in 1917, the Ministry of Food first considered a scheme of voluntary self-rationing in an attempt to deal with the growing shortage of staples such as bread, meat and sugar. The King himself led by example by implementing rationing on his own household. On 6 May 1917, his plea to his subjects to follow suit and be economical with food was read out in all the local places of worship. The response to this appeal from the sovereign of the land was the creation of the Bournemouth Food Control Committee, who in June 1917 posted to every household a 'Pledge' card together with an 'Honour Bound' card. Appealing to the patriotism of the public, it asked them to sign the pledge to economise with food, and also to display the 'Honour' card in their window, encouraging others to do the same. Over 11,000 homes in the Borough displayed their cards and agreed to the suggested restriction to their consumption of bread, meat and sugar. Due to the rising cost of bread, which reached one shilling in March 1917, posters went up exhorting the town to 'eat less bread', and in the run up to Christmas, newspapers were carrying adverts by the meat and milk suppliers warning of shortages in supply. Due to the restrictions placed on sugar, application forms were sent to each householder requiring them to register for a sugar 'ration card' at the grocer of their choice. Only those in possession of a card would be able to obtain 6oz of sugar per head, per week. It was possible to apply for extra sugar for jam making, however, anyone caught falsifying their application would be subject to a fine.

Eventually, the effects of this locally enforced system of rationing began to be felt in the hotels and restaurants in the town. The Regulation of Meals Order allowed them only to be able to provide a 3-course meal between 6 p.m. – 9 p.m., followed by another order requiring Wednesdays to be 'meatless' days, and potatoes to be only served on Wednesdays and Fridays. In 1918, as the shortages grew, meatless days would be increased to two per week. Christmas 1917 was a very subdued affair as the German U-boat campaign against the merchant ships hit hard. The items of traditional fayre essential to a good Christmas were in short supply, and obtaining ingredients such as margarine and chocolate meant joining the end of a long queue.

In February 1918, the Food Control Committee, aware that further imposed restrictions were needed to control the supply of basic foodstuffs, issued food cards to every household. These cards, one for butter, margarine and cheese, and another for meat and bacon were issued at Holy Trinity Church, Old Christchurch Road on receipt of a completed application form. Proving so successful that the queues across the town disappeared, these food cards were replaced nationally in October 1918 by ration books, thought to have been the brainchild of Bournemouth resident Miss Emily Sidebotham. Each ration book issued was only for use at the grocers where it had been registered. Inevitably, along with the original rationed items, tea and coal soon joined the growing list of items included in the book.

Anyone found cheating the ration book system, by altering the entries made in pencil, could face either a fine of up to £100 or six months' imprisonment. Government posters encouraged families to save food in order that there would be more available to feed the troops defending the country overseas. A *Win the War Cookery Book* published by the Food Economy Campaign contained recipes for creating alternatives such as barley bread, which were approved by the Ministry of Food.

In April 1918, two National Food Kitchens were set up in the working-class areas of Springbourne and Winton to deal with the issue of food shortages. Not to be considered as soup kitchens, the food was originally cooked on the premises and then sold as a 'takeaway'. Dining rooms were later provided where a full meal including pudding could be obtained for a reasonable price. The proof of their success and their popularity, not least to the growing workforce of women is evidenced in over 173,000 'takeaways' being sold during the first five months of operation. Although in February 1818 a third Food Kitchen was opened in Boscombe, all the kitchens closed on 22 May 1920. The site of the Winton Kitchen would later become home to the Workshops for the Disabled

Soldiers and Sailors.

The 7 January 1918 edition of *People's Friend* magazine published a recipe for War Cake requiring 'very little fat and NO eggs'

War Cake

5 ½ oz each of sugar, raisins, currants
1 tsp cinnamon
1 tsp ground ginger
½ tsp ground nutmeg
3 oz margarine
10 ½ oz plain flour
1 tsp bicarbonate of soda, ½ tsp baking powder, pinch of salt
Place all ingredients apart from flour, bicarb of soda & baking powder in saucepan with a pint of water and boil for 3 mins. Leave to get cold. Preheat oven. Grease & line a 2lb loaf tin. Add bicarb of soda & baking powder to flour and mix together. Sieve into cold mixture & stir well. Transfer mix to tin and bake for 1 hr or until skewer inserted into middle comes out clean.

Bournemouth 'Member's Food Card' Share No. 6996 (see main photo)

This card for the provision of rationed food, together with the earlier card for just butter and margarine is made out to the Hutchings Family for use in their registered grocers, the No. 8 Highfield Branch of the Parkstone & Bournemouth Cooperative Society. This relief depot stood at what in 1918 was 408 Wimborne Road, Moordown (now number 776), on the corner of Ensbury Park Road. The three members of the family were:

Percival Edward Hutchings born 1891, Lytchett Minister
Amelia Rose Barrett born 1895, Moordown
William F born 1917, Moordown

Percival and Amelia married in 1916, and were living in Nursery Road, Moordown where Amelia was born, when the cards were issued in 1918. Amelia's brother Sidney George Barrett enlisted in the Gloucester Regiment and was killed on 18 April 1918. He is remembered on the Tyne Cot Memorial.

(Author's Collection)

Inside Ration Card used by the Hutching's Family

As the cards show, not only were butter, cheese, and tea among the items subject to rationing, but also included were matches, soap and candles. That no potatoes appear to have been marked on the card from July to October, presumably indicates that the Hutchings family were amongst the other families doing their bit for the war effort and supplementing their diet by cultivating their back gardens.

'Don't Waste Bread!
Save two slices every day and Defeat the 'U' Boat'

British WW1 Poster

17 Theatre Royal Theatre Programme

September 1918

Entertainment: Morale: Tourism: Life in the Town

Britain declared War on Germany on Tuesday 4 August 1914, at the height of the holiday season for seaside towns dependent on the tourist trade. Initially there was a degree of panic in Bournemouth, with a number of visitors cancelling their bookings, banks closing for a few days and panic buying in some food shops. After the initial shock, life and the holiday season began to return to normal. By Christmas 1914, when realisation that invasion by Germany was not imminent, Bournemouth's visitors began to return in their numbers. Boarding houses and hotels reported full occupancy, and the pantomime 'Mother Hubbard' at the Theatre Royal played to packed houses. Everyone was confident that the war would not last long, but while it did and the reality of it remained unknown, people would continue to be entertained as usual. Although the proposal for the building of the new 'Pavilion' had been approved, work could not start for the duration of the war. However, there were still many places in the town catering for both holidaymakers and local theatre goers alike – the Theatre Royal, Boscombe Hippodrome and Winter Gardens, to name but three. Local venues played host not just to theatrical plays, but musical performances and silent movies. On 5 and 6 October 1914, the Theatre Royal, in Albert Road, played host to performances by the renowned ballerina Pavlova, and subsequently in 1915 the D'Oyley Carte Opera Company. Meanwhile, the Municipal Choir sang the Messiah at the Winter

THURSDAY
SEPTEMBER 12th

Thursday of this week is the opening day of a great

AUTUMN SALE

In the Arcade Departments of Bright's, an event providing almost innumerable money-saving opportunities in the purchase of Stationery, Silver and Electro Plate, Fancy Jewellery, Gold and Gem Jewelry, Trunks, Leather Goods, English and Foreign Fancy Goods of every description, Toys, Games, Sports Requisites of all kinds, Pictures and Prints, etc. Everything offered is of that high standard of quality ever associated with the name of "Bright's," and early purchase is strongly to be advised.

N.B.—The Gold and Gem Jewellery Department is a separate shop at the Southern Corner of the Arcade, facing the Pleasure Gardens.

BRIGHT'S

C.H. BEACH, Managing Director
The Arcade, Bournemouth
BOURNEMOUTH'S GREATEST STORE

If You want to SELL your Car TELL US, we have customers waiting
If You want to BUY a Car our second-hand list will appeal to you

The Southern Car Exchange
48, POOLE ROAD   Phone 806
H. G. CAPULE-WALKER   Principal

SCHOOL OF MODERN LANGUAGES

English, French, German, Italian, Portuguese, Russian, Spanish, etc.

Theatre Royal
BOURNEMOUTH

Sole Proprietor
Sole Lessee   GENEVIEVE WARD
Resident Manager   Sylvia Sunbar

MONDAY, SEPT. 9th, for SIX NIGHTS at 7.15.
Matinees Wednesday and Saturday at 2.

MACDONALD & YOUNG Present

... THE BOY ...

The New Musical Comedy, in Two Acts. Founded on Sir Arthur Pinero's Farce, "The Magistrate," now playing to Crowded Houses at the ADELPHI THEATRE, LONDON.

S. H. PARSONS
& Co.

CURRIERS,
LEATHER and
GRINDERY
MERCHANTS.

196 and 198,
Christchurch Rd.,
BOSCOMBE.

Prices

Wanted for Cash.

Send your News and Waste Paper, Rags, Bones, Iron, Skins, Brass, Copper, Zinc, Lead, Rubber, Kitchen Fat, Bags, Bacon Wrappers, Bottles & Jars to

NEWELL
WOLVERTON ROAD,
Boscombe   Christchurch

The South Coast.
Twilight Sleep MATERNITY HOME
"LANRICK,"
PERCY ROAD BOSCOMBE

Gardens, a venue that earned a reputation over the years for its excellent acoustics.

Cinema, although still somewhat in its infancy was fast catching up with the theatre, especially as a way to reach the masses. Bournemouth born Mrs Desmond Humphrey's film entitled '1914' became a very successful recruiting propaganda tool when it was shown to audiences at the Electric Cinema in Commercial Road. The Westover Palace screened the hit silent movie 'Morals of Marcus' during its run in 1915. Many of the new plays written and performed during the years of WW1 became a channel for propaganda, with stirring, emotive titles such as 'The Peril in our Midst' (1915) and 'For My Country' (1917). Theatre productions and the newly burgeoning film industry were keen to portray the values that the 'brave young men' were fighting (and dying) for. By special arrangement with the Exchange Telegraph, the latest war news was shown as soon as it was received at the Bournemouth Electric Theatre, who were also allowed to show the latest war films released by the censor.

Entertainment of all genres was seen as an important rehabilitation therapy for the wounded soldiers in the town, and from the beginning of their stay in local hospitals, the men were treated to special performances, particularly so at Christmas. During the Christmas of 1916, the actors from the pantomime 'Sleeping Beauty' at the Theatre Royal performed for 1,000 soldiers from all the local hospitals. Not only were the seats free of charge, but transport was provided and chocolates and cigarettes distributed. Entertaining the wounded continued throughout the war, contrary to some rumours that not only the wounded but those billeted in the town, were not welcome. After the war, the Commandant of one local hospital, stated that he felt certain that the thirty free seats each Friday at the Boscombe Hippodrome and free admission to the Winter Gardens had been 'one of the principal features in the recovery of the wounded'.

Maintaining a full programme of entertainment throughout the war years was, however, not without its obstacles. The lack of young male actors restricted the choice of play able to be staged, and after 1916 the Entertainment Tax prompted a rise in ticket prices, all of which, when added to the lighting restrictions in the town's public places and trams no longer running after 10 p.m., caused headaches to the theatre companies determined to keep the morale of troops and citizens at its highest. One practice implemented by the Theatre Royal was to commence its evening performances at 7 p.m., an hour earlier than usual, in order that patrons could catch the last tram home.

(Author's Collection)

Interior of Theatre Royal Postcard

Performers used their spare time to attend several fundraising events, and when called upon were more than happy to entertain for charitable causes. In April 1916, a benefit matinee was held at the Boscombe Hippodrome for 'Blinded Heroes', and the same year Hippodrome performers attended the Crag Head Hospital Garden Fete.

For the first time, the public were made aware of the horrors taking place in France, with the screening in September 1916 of, 'The Battle of the Somme'. News of the battle had been kept from those back home, and cinemas across the country were packed with people witnessing actual footage from the front. Bournemouth born Private Horace Ham attended the screening in the town with his father. Wounded whilst going over the top with the Middlesex Regiment on the morning of 1 July 1916, he later recalled vainly looking for any of his lost pals amongst the faces of the smiling men.

Dan Godfrey, later to become Sir Dan Godfrey, musical director and conductor, understood the value of music and entertainment in war time. While increased rail fares and the impact of military service had brought about a drop in visitors to the town, the wages earned by the female workforce, particularly those in munitions, more than compensated. Young women rejoiced in having money in their pockets, and determined to enjoy their new-found independence, booked frequent weekend breaks in the town. To provide them with first class entertainment and to keep them coming back to Bournemouth, Dan Godfrey booked top entertainers such as Vesta Tilley and George Robey to appear at the Winter Gardens during 1917. In the same year, in order to save paper, large posters were forbidden, therefore, theatres like the Winter Gardens and the Theatre Royal advertised their forthcoming attractions on painted canvas attached to hoardings across the town.

Nationally, there was divided opinion about theatrical entertainment continuing to provide fun and amusement when the newspapers were full of the horror happening on the battlefields of the Western Front and beyond. To some it was considered in bad taste and frivolous. However, in September 1918, the *Bournemouth Graphic* answered the criticism by suggesting that due to the 'splendid news from the front coming as a 'shimmering tonic', a great weight had been lifted from the public's shoulders and they were once again ready to enjoy the pleasure of entertainment. Nevertheless, plays such as 'The Luck of the Navy', staged by the Theatre Royal in August 1918, with its plot of a British Sub-Lieutenant spying for Germany, met with criticism from the censor - 'the general talk about the efficiency of Germans spies does not tend to have a useful effect.' In the end, the therapeutic and escapist benefits of all forms of entertainment during the war, from concert parties to hilarious revues were fully accepted, and the theatre and cinema proved to be invaluable tools of propaganda for the war effort.

'The love of fun is eternal and it will take a bigger beast than the Prussian to bully us out of it.'

The Bystander

18 'Death Penny'

Second Lieutenant Walter Percy Baker

Remembrance: Memorials: Local Lives

After the end of the First World War, Memorial Plaques, which came to be known as the 'Death Penny' or 'Dead Man's Penny' were issued from 1919 until the 1930s to the next-of-kin of all killed as a result of the war whilst serving with the British or Empire Forces.

Following a decision in 1916 by the British Government to create a lasting memorial for the families of those who gave their lives in the service of their country, a committee in 1917 agreed that the memorial should take the form of a bronze plaque bearing the name of the serviceman killed, to be accompanied by a memorial scroll. The design for the plaque would be the winning entry to a national competition announced in the *Times* on 13 August 1917.

'War Memorial for Next-of-Kin
Government Prizes for the Best Design'

The competition was open to British born subjects only, and the rules stated that the designs could be either circles or squares of 4 ½ ins or a rectangle of 5ins x 3 ½ ins. Apart from an instruction that the designs should be 'essentially simple and easily intelligible' the only additional stipulation was that the inscription 'HE DIED FOR FREEDOM AND HONOUR' should be included. The original closing date was given as 1 November, but this was subsequently

amended to 31 December 1917. Each of the 800 designs submitted to the National Gallery was given a pseudonym to ensure parity, and to avoid any suggestion of favouritism, the competing artist's name being held in a sealed envelope. In January 1918, the entry *Pyramus* was judged the eventual winner of a first-place prize of £250, the designer Edward Carter Preston also being awarded a second first place prize for an alternative design. Runner-up William McMillan would go on to design both the British War Medal and the Victory Medal.

Carter Preston's design is full of the symbolism one would expect from the Edwardian Imperialistic mentality of the time. The central figure Britannia stands together with a striding lion and holds in her right hand a trident, symbolising Britain's power and naval dominance. The laurel wreath, held by Britannia above the box containing the name of the deceased represents Victory. Given that when the competition was judged in 1917 this was by no means assured, it served to confirm the nation's conviction of 'The Triumph of Right Over Might'. Every part of the Death Penny has meaning, from the smaller lion biting the eagle, (Imperial Germany often represented by an eagle), to the dolphins swimming round Britannia emphasising again Britain's dominance at sea. British values of strength and endurance over adversity are portrayed with an oak branch and acorns. The name of the deceased would be added to the plaque in raised letters, but only the full name was allowed. The decision not to include the rank reflected the equality of the sacrifice made by all. As a final touch, Edward Carter Preston's initials appear above the front paw.

Production of the first of 1.3 million plaques began in December 1918 at the Memorial Plaque Factory at 54/56 Church Road, Acton, London. Each plaque had to be individually cast, and each name built up from separate letters. In all 450 tons of bronze would be needed to complete this massive undertaking. The majority of plaques made at the Acton factory can be identified by a small number behind the back leg of the striding lion, although the earliest of the Acton plaques was not numbered.

In December 1920, manufacture of the 'Dead Man's Penny'

moved to the Royal Arsenal at Woolwich which also took on the production of plaques for women when it was realised they would be needed. This resulted in a slight change to the design by way of narrowing the letter H in 'HE' to allow for the insertion of an S to read 'SHE'. Eventually, after approximately 1,500 had been produced in this way, the moulds were modified allowing for production of the male plaques by removing the 'S'. 600 plaques are inscribed for women who died during the war. Plaques manufactured at Woolwich can be identified by a WA stamped in a circle on the reverse and by the number being found between the tail and the leg of the lion, allowing for higher numbers than was possible previously.

These beautifully designed plaques and their accompanying scrolls were mostly well received by the next-of-kin of the deceased and played a symbolic part in the grieving process. It is worth noting here that the families of those soldiers executed during the war did not receive a memorial plaque. There was a strict order of precedence as to who should receive the plaque, starting with widow/widower down to the eldest living aunt on the mother's side. After the widow/widower, the male relative took precedence over the female, thereby the father would receive the plaque rather than the mother, and the eldest son before the eldest daughter.

Post war homes would find many of the memorial plaques given pride of place, some displayed in simple wooden frames, but others in elaborate, well-crafted surrounds, families drawing comfort from a tangible memorial to their loved one and representative of the headstone they would never get to see.

Second Lieutenant Walter Percy Baker was born in Weymouth in 1888 to Henry, a civil servant, and Eliza Ann, but by 1901 the family which now included six boys and one girl had moved to 'Ellerslie', 31 St Pauls Road, Bournemouth. In 1911, Walter was earning a living as an accounts clerk. Walter's service records no longer exist, although his medal index card indicates that he was originally a Corporal, regimental number 767 with the Hampshire Regiment, but in 1915 received a Commission to the 3rd Dorsetshire Regiment, under which his medals and Memorial Plaque would be issued. However, it would appear from Regimental records that the 3rd Dorsets did not see service overseas, therefore it was whilst subsequently attached to the Royal Warwickshire Regiment, 7th Battalion, that Walter landed in France on the 28 June 1916.

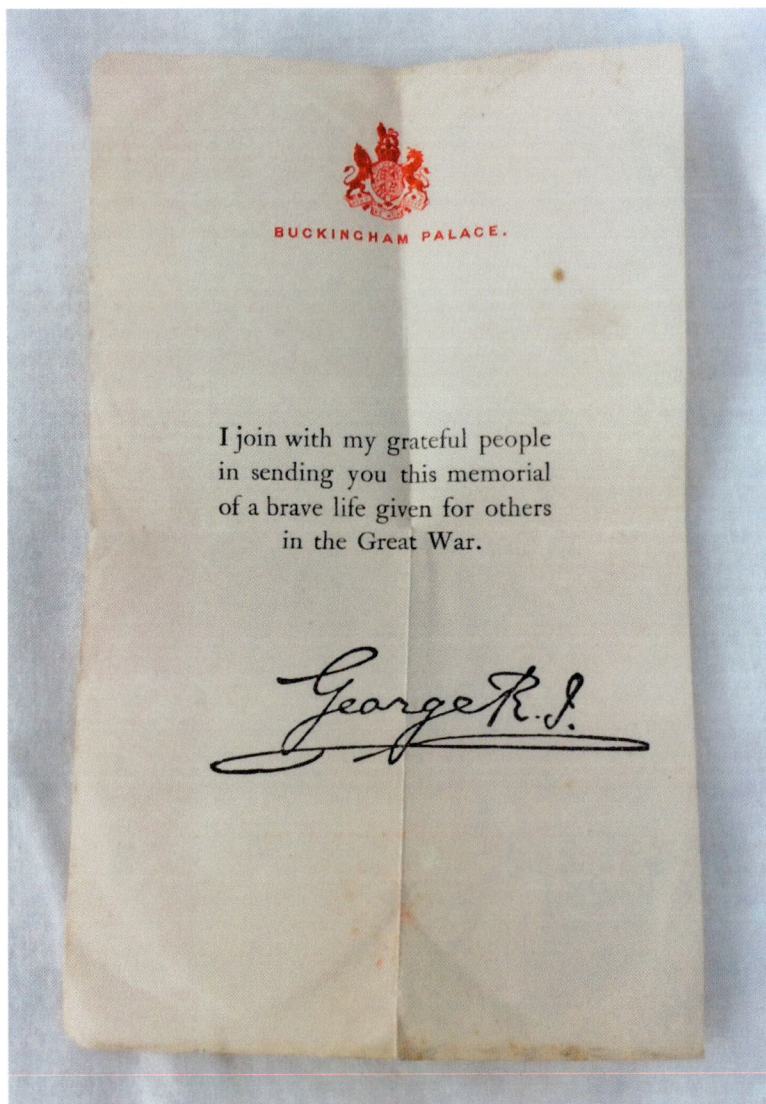

BUCKINGHAM PALACE.

I join with my grateful people in sending you this memorial of a brave life given for others in the Great War.

George R.I.

Letter Accompanying Death Plaque

The Battle of the Somme began on 1 July 1916 and as part of this larger offensive, the Battle of Bazentin Ridge took place from 14 to 17 July. The British 4th Army attacked the German 2nd Army at dawn in order to capture Ovillers, and whilst a French commander dismissed it as 'an attack organised for amateurs by amateurs' it was a success, despite a significant number of casualties. During the night of 13/14 July, the Reserve Army, X Corps, which included the 48th South Midland Division, and therefore the 7th Royal Warwickshire Regiment, continued to attack Ovillers. It was whilst attacking on 14 July that Second Lieutenant Walter Percy Baker was killed, just 2 weeks after first landing in France. The life of a junior officer on the Western Front was certainly a short one. It is thought that fifty men of the 7th Royal Warwicks died during that attack, including two further Second Lieutenants, one of whom, John Victor Jones, was also from the 3rd Dorsets. Bournemouth's Sydney Henry Thrift, serving as a Second Lieutenant with the Cheshire Regiment, was also killed that day.

One of Walter's brothers, Frederick Charles saw service with the RAF, and another, Arthur Harold, originally with the Hampshire Regiment, transferred to the Tank Corps as an engineer where he was awarded the MC and Bar. Both brothers survived the war.

Second Lieutenant Walter Baker is remembered on the Thiepval Memorial in France. Known as the Memorial to the Missing of the Somme, it remembers more than 72,000 men of the United Kingdom and South African forces who died in the area of the Somme before March 1918. Nearly 90 per cent of those inscribed on the memorial died during the Battle of the Somme (1 July 1916 – 18 November 1916) and have no known grave. Walter Baker is also remembered in his home town on the Memorial at St Swithin's Church, Bournemouth. His Memorial Plaque pictured here, in the original bespoke frame obtained by his grieving family was found in a house in Methuen Road.

(Courtesy of Rod Arnold)

Thiepval Memorial

'In splendid sleep, with a thousand brothers'

The Cenotaph by Charlotte Mew

19 Bournemouth Peace Medal

Armistice: Life in the Town: Commemoration

The signing of the Armistice on 11 November 1918, bringing to an end the fighting of the First World War, was greeted in the town of Bournemouth, as in all the towns across the Country, with great jubilation and rejoicing. Four long hard years had come to an end, and although recriminations and grief would follow later, that Monday morning was a day of celebration. At 10 a.m. The Mayor of Bournemouth proclaimed the news, outside the council offices in Yelverton Road, that there had been an agreement between Great Britain, France and Germany to enter peace negotiations and that the Armistice would come into force at 11 a.m. Officially, the 'war to end all wars', would only be over at the signing of the Treaty of Versailles on 28 June 1919, but the finer details did not matter to the townsfolk of Bournemouth. Within hours of the proclamation the town was festooned with bunting and the flags of the Allies. As the bells of St Peter's pealed loudly, crowds flocked to the streets waiving their Union Jacks, rode on the roofs and bonnets of horn-honking cars, and danced, cheered, and sang. Everyone wanted to join in the celebrations, so offices and shops closed early, and schoolchildren were let out of school in the afternoon in order to attend a special service of Thanksgiving held in the square at 1 p.m., led by The Mayor and The Bishop of Winchester.

'I ask the whole of the residents and visitors, in their rejoicings, to carry them out in a dignified manner, and one which will be a credit to the Borough of Bournemouth'

His Worship The Mayor

'This is a glorious day – a day glorious beyond all expectations, that has come now at last, suddenly as in a dream – a day that those who come after us will look back to and talk of'

The Bishop of Winchester

At the end of the service, the crowds joined in singing 'Old Hundredth', 'O God Our Help In Ages Past' and the National Anthem. Cheers rang out for the Prime Minister, David Lloyd George, Sir Douglas Haig and the whole of the British Forces while The Marseillaise and 'Rule Britannia' played. That evening, after services at St Peter's and other local churches, black out screens were finally removed, and the town was illuminated with lanterns and fireworks as people celebrated 'with dignity' into the night.

As the new year of 1919 began, plans got underway for marking the official end to the war later that year. The town was beginning to take on a markedly different look to that of the last four years. Soldiers billeted in the town had returned home, the remaining Belgian refugees were repatriated, and the auxiliary hospitals emptied as the wounded were moved to other hospitals. Many of the annual sporting events, such as tennis and bowls tournaments returned as life began to resume an air of normality. The holidaymakers once again crowded Bournemouth's beaches and packed the cinemas and theatres.

Peace Day, 19 July 1919 was an official day of celebrations across the country and in most commonwealth countries to mark the ending of the First World War. In London, thousands of people poured into the capital to take part in the Victory March.

Approximately 15,000 troops, led by the victorious Allied commanders marched through London on that Saturday morning passing the temporary wood and plaster Cenotaphs lining the route, erected to the memory of the fallen. Across the country, towns held their own Peace Day celebrations many including a parade of local schoolchildren and dignitaries.

In Bournemouth, despite bad weather that saw the postponement of several planned events, a service was held in Meyrick Park. Children from all the town's schools paraded through the town to the park, where they were presented with a souvenir Peace Medal by The Mayor to commemorate the ending of The Great War.

(Author's Collection)

Bournemouth Children Parading circa 1911

While some are generic in design, there are around 280 different Peace Medals to be found, representing the town or city where they were presented. Many, as with the Bournemouth medal, feature the winged Angel of Peace holding a laurel wreath, while others depict Britannia or a dove, another common symbol of peace. The

131

Bournemouth Peace Medal also features a soldier and sailor joining hands over the barrel of a gun. Nearly all the medals found were intended to be worn in some manner, the majority attached to a patriotic strip of red, white and blue ribbon, which in turn attached to a simple safety pin.

(Author's Collection)

Armistice Tin Badge c1919

In 2014, to mark the centenary of the outbreak of the First World War, the committee planning the Bournemouth commemorations, agreed to commission a new 'Peace Medal' to be presented to school children taking part in the Children's Festival on 24 July, held once again in Meyrick Park. Led by The Mayor in a horse drawn carriage, the participating children marched in a parade from the town's square to the park, just as children had done a hundred years before. Four thousand of the new peace medals were struck, using the design of the original. The new medals were double the size and thickness of the original, and were attached to a blue and yellow lanyard, Bournemouth's town colours. During the four years of Centenary Commemorations these new medals have also been given out to adults and children taking part in the various events that marked the ending of the First World War

'Gives somewhere back the thoughts by England given;
In hearts at peace, under an English heaven'

Rupert Brooke

20 Book of Remembrance

Remembrance: Memorials

The immediate sense of euphoria and celebration that 'the war to end all wars' was finally over naturally evolved into a determination and need to honour those who had left the town naively excited about the adventure ahead, but who paid the inevitable price of war. As early as 1917, shrines to honour the dead of the parish had begun to appear at several local churches, as either wall memorials inside or stone crosses in the grounds, often paid for by the families of those honoured. After the signing of the Armistice, public buildings and places of work felt the need to remember the staff who would not be coming home. However, in June 1919, a public meeting was held to consider the options for one focal point for the town's grieving families. At this meeting it was decided that in addition to building homes for the disabled soldiers who returned, a permanent memorial would be erected in the centre of the town, which would epitomise the pride Bournemouth felt for its war dead. Although there was a feeling among some that given the number of named memorials already placed in churches and work places, a specific town memorial was not necessary, a decision was finally made and the design by the Deputy Borough Architect, Mr E Shervey became a reality. The unveiling of the Bournemouth War Memorial took place on 8 November 1922 in the gardens facing the Town Hall. Unlike some town memorials, it has no names inscribed on it, the preference being for a single dedication on the bronze plaque:

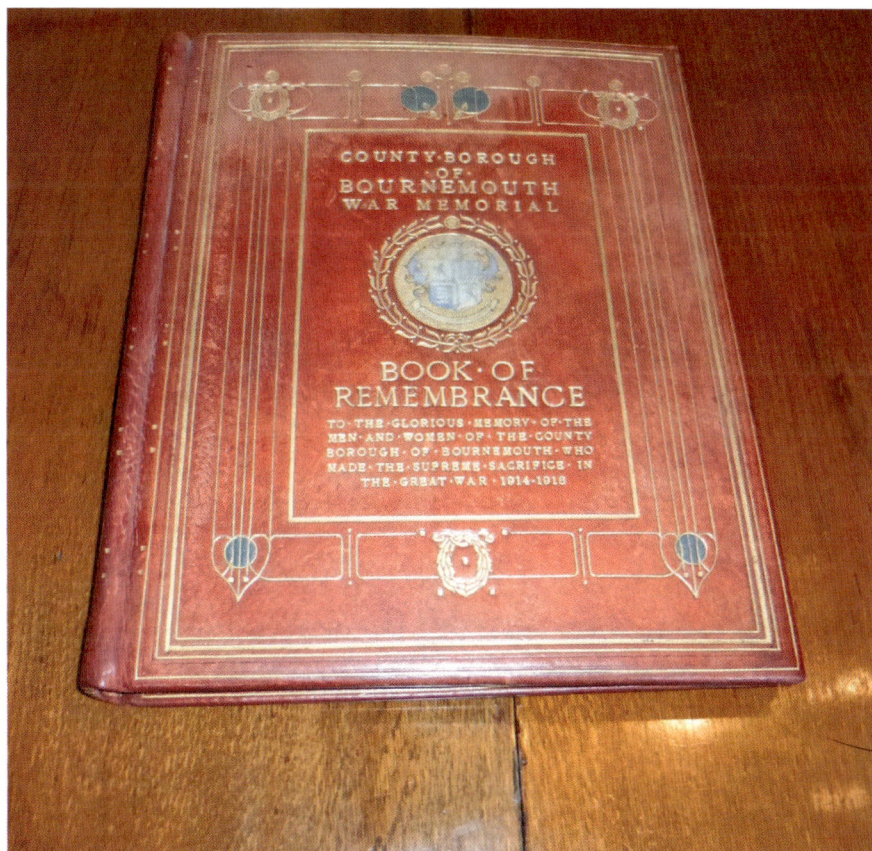

'To the Glorious Memory of those Men and Women of the County Borough of Bournemouth who made the Supreme Sacrifice in the Great War 1914 -1918'

The War Committee opted instead to record the names of the town's men and women in a Book of Remembrance. Contact was made with the local churches and religious organisations asking for the names of members of their parish who had been lost during the war. To reach those families who may not have attended a place of worship, adverts were placed in the local newspapers. In all 650 names were submitted, and entered on vellum in the leather-bound book, now kept in a locked shrine in the Town Hall.

These selective methods of obtaining the names of those killed during the war years did not lead to a totally comprehensive list. There are a number of possible reasons why eligible names were not submitted; a widow may have remarried; families moved away; illiteracy; or just a desire to put the war and the grief behind. The shortcomings in relying on these as a way of compiling a complete list became apparent in 2013, when the author began researching the memorial on the wall in St John's Church, Moordown. There are 118 names of local men inscribed on this memorial, and research on those from Moordown alone flagged up twelve that were not recorded in the official Book of Remembrance. In 2014, the author was given the opportunity to meet with The Mayor, Dr Rodney Cooper, who after viewing the evidence presented to him, agreed to add the missing twelve names to the addendum of the original book.

The author continued the research in order to compile a more accurate register of the town's casualties during the years 1914-1918. By cross-checking all records available at the time i.e. Commonwealth War Graves Commission database, Ancestry UK Military database and Census records, the eligibility for inclusion was established of a further 572 men and women, who had either been born or had resided in the town of Bournemouth. Casualties from parts of the town such as Kinson, not part of Bournemouth at the time of the First World War were not included in the original book, and therefore likewise in the later research. In keeping with the date specification on the 1920s Book of Remembrance, only those killed during the years 1914 – 1918 were added to the new register of names, despite the date of death of some named in the original book being as late as 1920. The author's main criteria for inclusion in any updated register of names was that there was a provable connection to Bournemouth, and this inevitably meant that some names found on church war memorials were not accepted. It was often the case that a family member moving into the area during the post war years wanted a permanent memorial to their loved one in the place they went regularly to worship, despite the man himself having no connection to the town.

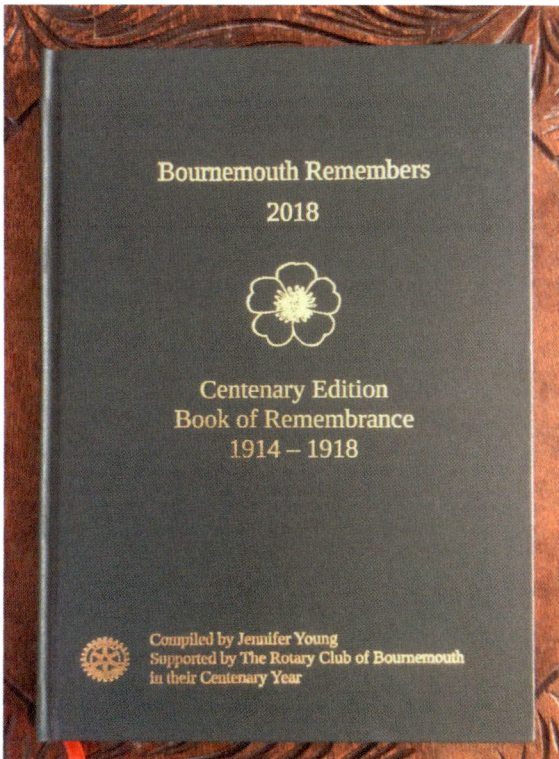

In 2018, when all available resources had been exhausted, and as a suitable commemoration to the hundred years since the signing of the Armistice, The Rotary Club of Bournemouth sponsored the publication of an updated Centenary Book of Remembrance. 'Bournemouth Remembers' contains the names of 1222 men and women who lost their lives during The First World War. None of the original 650 names have been omitted. The author does not make any claim that this new list is definitive. There will always be some who were missed, or whose details could not be proven at the time, but it is hoped that it goes someway to address the original omission and that regardless of rank or class, the sacrifice of those who called Bournemouth their home is remembered in perpetuity.

The new Book of Remembrance can be viewed at St Peter's Church, Bournemouth Central Library or the Dorset History Centre in Dorchester.

'He is not missing – he is here'

Field Marshall Lord Plumer

(Author's Collection)

1222 Poppy Cross Planting 11 November 2018

Bibliography

Books

Bloomfield, H., St John The Baptist, Parish History (1920)
Caunt, P. M., Military Sweetheart Jewellery, Pt 1., (Arbras 1994)
Cole, K., Postcards From the Front, (Amberley Publishing 2016)
Daybell, P., With A Smile and A Wave, (Pen and Sword Aviation 2014)
Edgington, M. A., Bournemouth and the First World War, (Bournemouth Local Studies 1985)
Mitrovic, A., (2007), Serbia's Great War 1914 – 1918, (Purdue University Press 2007)
Southall, R., Take Me Back to Dear Old Blighty, (Milestone Publications 1982)
The Bournemouth: The Magazine of Bournemouth School, Vol 3 April 1913 – December 1916

Oral History

www.iwm.org.uk: collections: sound: Horace George Ham (Oral History)

Newspapers

Bournemouth Graphic 1914 – 1919

Websites*

Allen, T., WW1 Penny-Flags and Flag-Days,
www.worldwar1postcards.com
Allen, T., Cigarettes & Tobacco and WW1 Soldiers,
www.worldwar1postcards.com
Cochrane, W., The Language of Stamps,
www.philatelicdatabase.com
Read, F., Look inside the Princess Mary Gift Fund 1914 Box,
www.iwm.org
Read, F., Trench Art, www.iwm.org
Stevens, S., Cigarette Silks – Military Textiles,
www.armymuseum.co.nz
Southam, H., The Bible and World War One – Women,
www.biblesociety.org.uk
20th (Light) Division History, www.en.m.wikipedia.org
Ancestry.co.uk/Census Records, www.ancestry.co.uk
Ancestry.co.uk/Military, www.ancestry.co.uk
Battle of Bazentin Ridge, www.en.m.wikipedia.org
Cenotaph, www.encyclopedia 1914-1918-online.net
Commonwealth War Graves Commission, Find War Dead,
www.cwg.org
Nursing during the First World War, www.VAD.redcross.org.uk
Peace Day 1919 – When The Boys Came Home – End of WW1,
www.forces-war-records.co.uk
Princess Mary Tin, www.collections.museumvictoria.com.au
Royal Warwickshire Regiment, www.forces-war-records.co.uk
The Comprehensive Guide to the Victoria & George Cross,
www.vconline.org.uk
The First Official Flag-Day, www.prisonersofwar1914-
1918documents.com
War Cake Recipe, January 7, 1918, www.thepeoplesfriend.co.uk
WW1 Memorial Plaque, www.researchingwww1.co.uk
* All consulted January 2019

Articles

Rabbetts, G., Angel of the Workshops

Printed in Great Britain
by Amazon